The Mouth that Roared

Praise for *The Mouth that Roared*

Les is a frontline urban lifesaver, rescuing the drowning from their addictions. If you want to know the truth about Australia, and what's gone wrong, *The Mouth that Roared* is a compelling read.

— Chris Smith, 2GB radio presenter

Les Twentyman is a legend, a true guardian angel in the wilds of Western suburbia where so many are forgotten or maligned. Filled with his characteristic humour, wit and knack for telling a good tale, this is a book that should be read by policymakers, politicians and opinion columnists. They might learn something from the Braybrook boy who didn't finish high school, but who truly understands the heart and humanity behind our most vulnerable and voiceless.

— Alice Pung, author

Les Twentyman is one of the gems of Melbourne life: the perfect example of good people who don't care where you come from or what you sound like. Les is authentic. He is passionate, he cares and he gets it more than just about anyone. His is a story of a bloke who enjoys a laugh, a good time and, by being non-judgemental towards everyone he meets, is able to connect disparate spirits and save lives. That's a story worth reading.

— Eddie McGuire AM, TV and radio presenter,
President, Collingwood Football Club

Les Twentyman's memoir is funny, honest and inspiring. His memories of growing up in the western suburbs are warm and wonderful. A restless student, most likely to disrupt classes with his constant questioning, he has built a life on challenging authority and raising his hand to talk on behalf of those who don't have strong voices. Through football, politics, community work and media, Les has been an outstanding leader and is one of Australia's great storytellers.

— Paul Kennedy, ABC TV presenter and author

Leslie Twentyman OAM is a prominent youth outreach worker and community activist in the western suburbs of Melbourne. Raised in Braybrook, he is one of Australia's best-known social campaigners on issues ranging from homelessness, drug abuse, prison reform and social welfare. In 1984, Twentyman and Ron Coleman, then owner of the *Western Times*, founded the **20th Man Fund** to give 10 young homeless people a Christmas party. Now **The Les Twentyman Foundation**, the fund has grown exponentially to become a vital resource for young people, dedicated to providing positive intervention and unconditional support to thousands of at-risk youth each year. In 1994 Les Twentyman received an Order of Australia; in 2004, he was a finalist for Australian of the Year; and in 2006, he was awarded Victorian of the Year.
www.20thman.com.au; www.ltfoundation.com.au

Robert Hillman is a Melbourne-based writer of over 60 works of fiction and non-fiction. His autobiography, *The Boy in the Green Suit*, won the Australian National Biography Award for 2005. His 2007 biography, *My Life as a Traitor*, written with Zarah Ghahramani, appeared in numerous overseas editions and was short-listed for the Prime Minister's Literary Awards in 2008. He wrote the best-selling *The Rugmaker of Mazar-e-Sharif* (2008) in collaboration with former Afghan asylum seeker, Najaf Mazari, followed by a collection of modern Afghan fables, *The Honey Thief*. In 2013, Robert's biography on Gurumul Yunupingu, *Gurumul: His Life and Music* (2013) was released to great acclaim.

The Mouth that Roared

A memoir

Les Twentyman
with
Robert Hillman

Published by Wild Dingo Press
Melbourne, Australia
books@wilddingopress.com.au
www.wilddingopress.com.au

First published by Wild Dingo Press 2017
Text copyright © Les Twentyman & Robert Hillman
The moral right of the author has been asserted.

Except as permitted under the Australian Copyright Act 1968, no part of this book may be reproduced, stored in a retrieval system, or transmitted in any form or by any means, electronic, mechanical, photocopying, recording, or otherwise without prior permission of the copyright owners and the publisher of this book.

Cover design: Emma Statham
Editor: Catherine Lewis
Typesetting: Midland Typesetters
Print in Australia by Ligare

National Library of Australia
Cataloguing-in-Publications Data

Twentyman, Les, 1948- author.
　　The mouth that roared / Les Twentyman and Robert Hillman.

　　ISBN: 9780987381361 (paperback)
　　ISBN: 9780987381378 (ebook: pdf)

　　Twentyman, Les, 1948-
　　Social workers—Victoria—Biography.
　　Social service—Victoria.
　　Other Creators/Contributors:
　　Hillman, Robert, 1948- author.

This book is dedicated to my wife Cherie, and granddaughter Lotus, who has lived with us for seven years; my late father and mother, Leslie Jack Snr and Ilma; my brothers Garry, Dennis, Mark, and sister Sandra.

Acknowledgements

Whatever I've achieved is only possible because of the dedication and long-term commitment of a wonderful team of people from all walks of life—those who took on the challenge to change their lives, those who work directly with and mentor our youth, those who have a big heart along with the influence or the cash to ensure the Les Twentyman Foundation continues to grow and give our youth at risk a real chance at life. So big cheers and thank yous to:

All the battlers, the young people whom my fellow youth workers—Jim, Richard, Sarha, Jana, Gum, Ben, Lisa and volunteers—work with every day to give them a pathway to a happy and fulfilled life.

I would also like to thank long-time supporters who have helped get this book to the starting line: Harold Mitchell, Rick Smith, John Fowler, Lloyd Williams, Bruce Mathierson Jnr, John Shore, Paul Wheelton AM, and his brother Simon; and in very recent times, Nick Johnstone and his wonderful, supportive family.

To all who have encouraged me to open up my life to the world: the master craftsman of writing, Robert Hillman, who as well as turning my outpourings into a book, was somebody on whom I could unload some of the Tough Stuff that has been bottled up for so long; my publisher at Wild Dingo Press, Catherine Lewis, for taking the book on; and former long-time *Herald Sun* columnist Bryan Patterson, who sparked the interest for a book four years ago.

Finally, to my board led by Dr David Young and Ros Andrews, our CEO Wayne Owens; and Club 20 members, without whom we could not function.

Hopefully this book will enlighten Australians of the tasks that lie ahead and inspire us all to tackle them like the Mighty Western Bulldogs did in 2016 when they showed the AFL sporting world that champions get up when they can't.

1

Junk

She might be thirty, a bit haggard, black T-shirt, black slacks, long dark hair. She's in charge of a baby in a stroller. She's just taken a seat in a park in Footscray, a ramshackle place, scraggly eucalypts, parched grass, rubbish in small windswept heaps. And amongst the rubbish, used sharps, cellophane syringe wrappers, plastic sterile water bottles—enough for one whack. The place has a name—MacNab Park, just a sliver of land, an exit from Footscray Station leading to it. I'm on my way from somewhere or other to the office of Open Family in Nicholson Street, a hundred metres away. That's where I work, at Open Family. This is 1995, twenty-four years ago, so I couldn't swear to what I'd been doing before I came upon this woman. What I would be able to swear to, though, is that whatever business I'm engaged in on this sunny Friday will have something to do with exactly what I'm looking at: an addict in a needy state, her priorities completely focused on scoring. And she's got another one of her kids with her to help the business along—a boy of five or six in shorts and a rumpled shirt and thongs. I stand where I am and watch. I know what's going to happen. She sends the kid running off to a dealer. Always dealers in this patch of Footscray, tucked away in the shadows, hands in pockets, vacant expression, but actually very alert. Very. And an addict knows exactly where to find him; every addict beyond a certain level of experience has a preternatural homing instinct. The dealer could be in a bunker twenty metres underground and an addict will sniff him out. Two minutes later, the kid comes running back, one hand clenched. He slips a little plastic baggie into his mum's hand, then stands glancing about: north, south, east and west. The woman has sent the kid because the cops might have the park under surveillance and a kid will attract less attention than an addled woman with a haunted look about her.

As I say, I'm watching as I shuffle along, the noise of the traffic on Dynon Road reaching me as a sustained roar. The woman doesn't pay any attention to me because she can tell, even at a distance, that I'm no threat to her. Addicts know at a glance if they have to be wary of this person or that, and they know who's harmless. I'm glad that she thinks of me as one of the harmless. Because I truly don't wish her any harm. I wish her exactly the opposite. I wish she had a comfy, middle-class home to go to, and a big Sony Trinitron television, and a welcoming bedroom for her son, and a monster, space-age Westinghouse refrigerator. And not only material stuff, also a husband who provided love and support, for instance; a job that yields a reliable income; a sense of purpose in life. These are just the normal aspirations of most of the adults in Australia, but she can't enjoy them. She's got heroin instead.

Yep, she's got the junk she needs, and she's got a spoon to mix it with the sterile water. She rapidly does what she has to do, puts the flame of a cigarette lighter under the bowl of the spoon, tears open the syringe packet with her teeth, draws up the slurry of dope into the sharp, squeezes her fist, brings up a vein, or what's left of a vein, sinks the needle expertly, sucks up some of her living blood into the syringe, injects. One, two, three, four, five, six, seven—whack. She's still sitting. Her head drops onto her chest. The kid stands there passively. The baby in the stroller is quiet.

I walk past her, my head bowed. After all I've seen in my time amongst the hopeless and addled, the broken, the put-upon, the helpless and homeless, those who struggle every day to stay alive, who'd believe I could still feel this much sorrow at the sight of a woman and her junk and her kids? But sometimes it gets to me as if I were witnessing distress of this sort for the first time. The first time. It truly does. I wish there was something I could take to make it all grow blurry—a type of heroin for the onlooker, nothing too devastating, just ten minutes of relief. But there isn't. You see it, you bow your head, you mutter a type of all-purpose prayer for the woman and her kids, and you get yourself across the street through the traffic into the Open Family office and make yourself a cup of tea, good strong tea, a bit of milk. And that's it.

But why didn't I intervene? Why didn't I go over to the woman and say: "Listen, you need to take a good, hard look at yourself". Because I don't do that. I never have, and I hope to God I never will. On top of everything else she's dealing with, what would be served by me ripping into her? The time will come when I'll have something to say to her. It won't be censorial. It'll be: "Where're you sleeping tonight, sweetheart? You've got somewhere? Anything to eat, you and the kids?"

A few years ago, Susie Williams and Paula Fox, the wives of Lloyd Williams and Lindsay Fox (don't pretend you haven't heard of them) asked me to take them around some of the meaner streets of the western suburbs and give them a first-hand look at the problems I deal with every day of the year. They'll be making a donation to the 20th Man Fund, the welfare, intervention and outreach organisation I founded way back then, and they want to know more. We go here and there, we get out of the car and walk, I indicate with a nod of my head where they need to direct their gaze, a kid of sixteen down an alley on the nod, a syringe hanging out of his arm; a woman huddled in the gutter, muttering to herself. You get the picture, no need to labour the point.

Susie and Paula, they're not shocked, but they're saddened, concerned, they've got the contacts to do some good, yeah, but they've also got something in their hearts that *makes* them want to do some good, which is the crucial thing. The thing is—and this is what I try to reveal to Susie and Paula—is that the so-called dark side of Melbourne, our city, the concealed side, especially the western suburbs, is not concealed at all, it's not in the shadows, it's out there on display, as plain as the Maccas on the corner, as the Woolies, the pizza parlour, the mums in their four-wheel drives ferrying the kids to school. Maybe we don't stop and gaze down an alley where some kid's doing his junk; maybe we stroll past the woman babbling in the gutter, but the kid and the woman are there, they haven't hidden themselves away. It's just that we say: "But that's not the real Melbourne, that's just a tiny part of something way bigger". What I've been on about for decades is that the kid and his junk, the woman with her scrambled brain are as much a reality as the shiny people of the city.

I'm in the office, I'm at my desk, I've got my cup of tea in my Bulldogs mug. I'm blue, just for the time being. That woman, the kid. I'm asking myself if it ever ends. Each person I find a way to help, two more appear. But I rouse myself—I have to, it's important. I say: "Jesus, Les, it's not footy. You don't win the premiership at the end of the season." You don't win anything. But what I have to believe is that I'm doing some good. And Les, if it wasn't you doing the job, it would have to be somebody else, wouldn't it?

I mean, bloody hell, someone's got to do it. Cuppa, a little pep talk, I'm okay again. What talents I have, they're exactly right for this job. I'm obstinate, so that's good, isn't it? I'm fairly thick-skinned, and that's important; there are lots of people about the place who want to sink the slipper. And I know bullshit when I hear it—you know, a pious government minister telling you that people have to take responsibility for their own lives, which is true, but not when they've got sexual abuse interfering with their ability to think straight. Okay, I'm the right bloke for the job. I accept that. I've got the pedigree. Some others have a pedigree that comes down to them from parents rich as stink, fancy private school, fabulous tailoring at Henry Bucks. My pedigree is working-class: parents who rolled up their sleeves and ran a fruit and vegetable shop in Braybrook; rough-and-ready government school; tailoring at Denny's Variety Store. I finish the cuppa, take a deep breath and ask Helen, who helps out in the office: "What's next?"

2
Standing Up

Five kids in the Twentyman family of Williamstown and Braybrook: four boys, one girl. Doesn't happen much these days, five kids in a family. Most parents, particularly the parents in the salubrious suburbs, the posh suburbs as you might term them—no, no, no. Two kids, call it stumps. But five little Twentyman champions, and that was nothing compared to my Dad's family of thirteen. Kids in huge families like that spend a lot of time correcting their parents.

"No, I'm Bobby, Dad, that's Herbie over there."

"Is that right?" says Dad. "Well, whoever you are, I need you to go down the shops and get me some Turf Filtereds. And don't smoke any of 'em on the way back, alright?"

Off goes Bobby, leaving Dad to work out the names of the other ten kids. You know, in a way, growing up in a family with herds of kids is the most human upbringing you can have, allowing that Mum and Dad can provide for you. It gives you a taste of give-and-take, and it teaches you not to give yourself airs, sell yourself as flash goods when deep down, you're just a human being. That's what I knew about myself—I was one of the Twentyman tribe, and each member of the tribe needed love and support. And they got it, the love and support. Okay, in a big family the parents are on the frontier of insanity a lot of the time, countless things to do, never a moment's peace; but that's human, too, the bustle and the shouting and the "Where're my socks? Mum, I can't find my socks!" All of that's good for the soul.

But listen. You'll remember I was talking about my working-class pedigree. You can add this to it: my dad fought on the Kokoda Trail. That's as high a commendation as Gallipoli. I was proud of him for what he did in the war. I didn't know as a little kid exactly what sort of achievement that was, fighting your way up and down the Owen Stanley Range, mud pouring through the ravines while the Japanese snipers were angling for a spot to put a bullet into your brain box. It takes character. Nothing I've done for the dispossessed and addled of the west can compare to what my dad did for his mates on the Kokoda, but at least it's been an inspiration to me. His name was Les Twentyman, same as me. Mum's name was Ilma, and she matched dad in strength of character. I said that the parents of big families are most of the time on the borderline of insanity. Well, that's especially true of the mother. She has to keep in her head a sort of psychological profile of all the kids, their frenzies and phobias, their troubles, their joys; has to act as a peacemaker at times, at other times chase them about uttering dire threats.

My mother knew exactly how to do all that, while at the same time running the household, keeping sugar in the canister, salt in the shaker, biscuits in the bikkie tin, milk in the fridge, seven dinner plates on the kitchen table. Keeping a family of hubby and five kids going, it's a bigger job than running GMH. (When we had a GMH, that is.) The most common expression on my mum's face when I was growing up was one of exhaustion kept at bay by gritty determination. At the same time, she could find a smile. And sometimes the complete opposite of a smile. I can remember back to when I was a little tacker of five, and Dad was supposed to take me to the footy after he'd met up with his Tobruk mates for an ex-army get-together of the 18th Brigade of the 7th Divie. Mum said: "Don't forget". The appointed time came around in the early arvo for Dad to collect me; no sign of him. Then Mum, wise to his dodges, looked over our back fence and saw him making his stealthy way through the long grass of the paddock behind us, towards the bus stop where he'd catch the bus to the footy ground. He was trying to avoid coming home because he knew Mum would guess the number of glasses of the chilled article he'd sampled. (A lot.) She grabbed me, hustled me out the back gate and across the paddock. The bus had just stopped and she was waving vigorously to make sure the driver saw her and waited. (He'd better, if he knew what was good for him.) She hoisted me up into the bus and instructed the driver thus: "This is Leslie, he's with the bloke hiding under the back seat".

I come from an enterprising family but my mum maybe deserved first prize as the most enterprising of all. She barely took a breather from the time of the birth of her first child (me) to the day she entered advanced old age. Sleeves rolled up, she was right in amongst it, running the household, helping out in Dad's greengrocer's shop, attending to crises amongst her neighbours. You might be thinking, "Okay, everybody has a good word for his or her mum," but listen to this tale. In my twenties, I owned a little Honda Scamp, not much oomph, and the day came when I got an opportunity to trade up to something grander—a Falcon—nice piece of machinery. The car came from my mate, David Thorpe, who ran a used car yard. He accepted the Scamp as a trade-in, sight unseen. When he came to pick it up from our place, it was discovered that one of the axles was broken.

"Bloody hell, Les, you're giving me a trade-in that I'll have to get a welder to work on before I can sell it. I thought you were my mate."

My mum emerged from the back door. She'd overheard the complaint.

"Keep your shirt on, Dave," she said. "I'll weld it." She was a very competent welder, my mum, and under the Scamp she goes, geared up with her mask, equipment in hand; has the axle in good order in no time.

The fruit and vegie shop my parents kept was in Churchill Avenue, Braybrook. Now, running a greengrocer's is no bed of roses. You're up early six days a week to get to the wholesale market in Footscray, load the back of the truck, off to Churchill Avenue by about 6 o'clock, raise the roller door, get the fruit on the display racks, the vegies all out on show. And if you keep at it day after day, week after week for the whole year, then yeah, you can just about make a living. Just about. But for my family and for every other working-class family in Australia back in the 1950s and 1960s, the life you lead was pretty much hand-to-mouth. No such thing as savings to fall back on. And the dole, if you couldn't keep up? Oh, dear. The dole. On the dole in those days, you got the opportunity to starve to death at a more gradual rate. Not everyone realises that Australia, for the working-class, was only a little bit above a third-world country in the 1950s. Most of what we call the social safety net didn't exist. No Medicare, no sickness benefits, no disability allowance. In Braybrook, your neighbours pitched in if you were doing it tough, lost your job, whatever. Your neighbours provided the safety net. Let's say you're struggling along, your job's gone down the gurgler, kids dressed by Vinnies. You meet a mate in the street and he's got a half pound of butter for you, slips it into your coat pocket: "Hope this helps," he says, gives you a pat on the shoulder, you go on your way. You meet another neighbour; he slips you a ten-bob note. "Look after yourself," he says. One fine day, you find another job, begin to build your life up again, the kids and the missus remember how to smile. And now you're the bloke who slips your mate a half-pound of butter when he loses his job; you're the bloke who murmurs: "Take care of yourself".

That generosity in working-class communities isn't there in this new millennium. At some point, it began to fade away. I suppose nowadays when people see someone struggling, they think: "Centrelink will look after him". Or maybe the Department of Human Services. Or maybe the Salvos. As pensions and other types of support have become more pervasive, the commitment of neighbour to neighbour has dwindled. I don't want to complain about that. After all, that's what we fought for, increased government support. But at the same time, it's sad. In 2017, nobody's going to slip a half pound of butter into your coat pocket. Nobody's going to say quietly: "You look after yourself, mate".

That generosity was there in my family, too; brother to brother; brother to sister. I had a paper round when I was a kid of about nine, up and down the streets of Braybrook on my *Malvern Star* with *The Sun News Pictorial* and *The Age* (far fewer copies than *The Sun* in a suburb like Braybrook—*The Age* was the newspaper of the middle class; *The Sun* was for the working class) to pop into letterboxes. Anyway, one cold and bitter morning, a real bastard, still dark, sleet in my face, the wind like a dagger—this morning, as I say, I'm out and about on my deliveries, huge stack of papers in a bag with two deep pockets, one hanging over each side of a rack behind me, my face red with the cold, fingers frozen on the handlebars. I'm pedalling away, dreaming of delivering the last paper, getting home to the warmth of our place on Myamyn Street. And I skid on the wet footpath, crash to the ground, the papers tumble out and go flying everywhere in the wind. My knees are skinned and bleeding and I'm howling my head off. Any paper I lose I have to pay for out of my own money, out of my earnings. That's why I'm howling. I struggle home to our house and find Dad, who's the only one up and about at that hour of the morning. Dad says: "What the hell happened to you, kiddo?" I pour out my tale of woe. Dad says: "We'll fix this". He rouses my brothers and my sister, rouses Mum, gets them all into the truck and up and down the dawn streets of Braybrook we go, gathering up the newspapers and delivering them. That's where I get my conception of what a family should be—from my Dad, my Mum, my brothers and sister. No complaints from any of them. No: "Gawd, Les, you're a pain in the arse." They knew they had to pitch in, and they did. You see what I'm looking for in the families I deal with in the west, or anywhere? I'm looking for that generosity, one to the other in a family. I want every family to show that concern. I want them all to be the Twentymans of Myamyn Street, circa 1958. But the thing is, it's only when it's not there that I become involved.

Now, Braybrook. I'm about to tell you about Braybrook. Because in the entire literature of the Commonwealth of Australia, no author has thought to honour my old suburb, say a few attractive things about it. Not in fiction, not in a history text, and certainly not in poetry. But Braybrook deserves better. It sits out there in the west between Ballarat Road and Sunshine Road, both running east and west. Churchill Avenue with its dogleg (where my dad's fruit and vegie shop was situated) and South Road run in between. You've got Duke Street and Ashley Street heading north and south, forming the boundary between Braybrook and Sunshine on one side; Braybrook and Maidstone on the other. Skinner Reserve is pretty much smack in the middle of the suburb—where you go for your footy and all of that sort of thing—little bit of greenery in a suburb not famous for its parks and gardens, I have to admit. Although across Ballarat Road, you run into the Maribyrnong River; there's a certain amount of greenery along this western bank but much more on the far side, the Avondale Heights side. I think we got dudded when they were drawing up the boundaries of these western suburbs; Braybrook should have been given both banks of the Maribyrnong. There's just the one bridge across the river from Braybrook to Avondale Heights—Solomon's Ford, where the goldseekers streaming out west to the Ballarat goldfields used to cross. One of the few historical sites in my old suburb.

Braybrook is, of course, working-class, like Footscray, Sunshine, Maidstone. But more so. Braybrook defines the

Melbourne working-class suburb. Nothing fancy about Braybrook, but I will say this—it's got heart, and it's got heart because it's seen so much struggle. I suppose it would be true to say that the heart was more in evidence when I lived there as a kid than today. The struggle in those days was simply the age-old battle of those without money to hold on, to stay afloat. It was a place of shared values, shared politics. Everyone knew a bloke or two who drank too much, but there was no heroin, no speed, no ice. Unless you're just totally ridiculous in your drinking habits, you can maintain a close relationship with the bottle and still make your living. But heroin?—Jesus Christ, no. Alcohol feeds into your veins more gradually than heroin. Your system can, with a bit of effort, accommodate it. But heroin is whack! Into your arm, seven seconds later the world has gone, ten minutes later, you're on the nod. And when you revive, you want it again—whack. No community can withstand widespread heroin use. At a certain time, I couldn't give you the exact year, the hardship in Braybrook stopped having much to do with old-fashioned working-class hardship and became, instead, the rack and ruin of hard drug use. If you're an addict, you haven't got much to share with anyone except other addicts. No addict is going to say to you: "Doing it tough, mate. I'm looking for employment, but it's not there." That's human, trying to find a job. You know what the bloke's talking about. You slip the half pound of butter into the coat pocket. But if the bloke mutters: "Doing it tough, mate. Need to score," what can you say? "Here's a hundred milligrams, take care of yourself." No.

In the Twentyman household in Myamyn Street there were certain expectations. You didn't make an excessive amount of trouble for your mum and dad; you pulled your weight; you refrained from murdering your brothers, your sister, no matter how annoying they might become; and you got yourself off to school. Which I did. Couldn't say I was crazy about school, but I went, and sat up straight in my desk, and did my lessons when I could find the wherewithal. Look, I want every kid in Australia to go to school and get an education, but at the same time I have to say that almost everything I know that means a damned thing, I learnt outside the classroom, on the streets, in the hurly-burly of relationships, at work, down the pub. It's my temperament. I'm not a sit-down learner. I'm an on-my-feet learner. Now, this is especially true when it comes to your heart. The best stuff you'll learn is what you learn with your heart. No teacher is ever going to get you to understand what human sympathy is, what love is, what decency looks like. I picked up all of that from my dad, my mum, my brothers and sister, my grandparents, about a dozen cousins, and from people I met knocking about Braybrook and the west. Let me provide an illustration. Everyone likes an illustration. Okay, think of my dad in his fruit and vegie emporium on Churchill Avenue. He meets all sorts every day. And one of the people he counts as a customer is a woman with six kids, Glenda, never known an easeful day in her thirty-six years. And one fine day Glenda comes into the shop with red eyes and a devastated look about her. Dad says: "Glenda sweetheart, what's your grief?" Glenda says: "My old man's bolted". Meaning, he's run out on his wife and his six kids, gone God knows where. Now, if your old man clears off, you're in strife. In the 1950s, it was a difficult thing for a woman to hold down a full-time job, bring in an income that could support one kid or two, let alone six. So being left as the sole source of support for your kids—it was a catastrophe. Glenda can't even think of keeping the six kids under one roof; she's going to have to farm them out to a children's home. It's likely to break her heart, but she hasn't got a choice. Dad says to Glenda: "We'll take Billy". Billy was the third of the six, about eleven years old—Dad had seen him with Glenda now and again. So, here's Dad with five kids to raise putting his hand up to act in the role of father for another one. And he got no grief from Mum. She accepted the burden without the slightest complaint. Me?—yeah, I had a few complaints. Billy was older than me, so I was no longer the most senior kid in the household. It made me feel that I'd been relegated to second place on the podium, my gold medal snatched away and given to someone else. And Billy was given the top bunk in our bedroom. The top bunk had been mine—it was a symbol of status to be in the top bunk. Not pleased. Did I mind my manners? I think so. Maybe not always.

At school one day, I was in a bad mood, full of grievance, and I told the other kids in the class and the teacher that Billy was a ring-in, not really a genuine Twentyman, a charity case. "He's not in our family. He's not my real brother." Why did I say this? Maybe it was just the spite that can get into your guts at times; something that leaves you ashamed of yourself later. Dad comes to hear about what I'd said at school and he gave me A Talking To. Yes, one of the classics, it was. And I remember it. He told me that I'd let him down, let the Twentyman family down by telling people that Billy was a ring-in. "It's our job to help that boy through this bad time, Les. Can't you see that? You've got a dad, and that's me, but Billy, his dad's gone bush, turned his back on him. Can you see how that would make a kid feel? That his dad doesn't want him?" Oh yeah, I was ashamed of myself. But all of this is by way of showing you what you learn in your home, from your dad. That's education, a talk like that. It got into my heart and changed the way I thought. I don't know if I can claim that anything I learnt in the classroom had that sort of influence on me. It's not when you hear someone talking that a lesson gets to you; it's when you see someone acting on what they say. People can say anything. But it's how they act that provides the proof. You know, at Christmas that time Billy was with us, all of us kids were given watches as presents. This was a substantial sort of present, a wristwatch, long before the digital era when you could buy a hundred watches for five hundred dollars if you liked, things manufactured in some vast factory in the backlots of the People's Republic of China. These were the genuine article, genuine clockwork inside. And Billy was given a watch, too. With my dad, if you were in, you were in, you weren't half in and half out.

Sunshine East Primary—that was my first school. If I say to anyone these days: "My primary school was called Sunshine," they think I must be talking about some sort of proto-hippy experimental place. But there you go. 'Sunshine' has to be understood ironically, because the sunshine that reached Sunshine itself had to make its way down through a thick layer of smoke and smog. It's an industrial suburb, Sunshine, the one-time site of the biggest industrial plant in Australia, the Sunshine Harvester Works. The suburb used to be Braybrook Junction but it was changed to 'Sunshine' back in 1907 to honour H.V. Mackay, who started up the harvester company. He was a bit of a visionary, old H.V; he owned 400 acres at Sunshine and he set to work to build a workers' town, what the German socialists of that time called a 'Siedlung', designed from the ground up to provide workers with somewhere they could thrive. It was like a self-contained community with a medical clinic, child-minding facilities, small parks and playgrounds, and a school. And compact modern houses for the entire workforce of the harvester plant. Old H.V. wanted all of his workers to live locally, partly because of the convenience and partly because he was a bit of a feudal lord deep down and he saw Sunshine as his fiefdom—but a sort of benevolent fiefdom, all the workers jolly and satisfied, calling out to H.V. as he took his morning walk about the place: "Good morning, chief! Good to see you, chief! God bless you, chief, and your lovely wife and gorgeous kids! May you live for an eternity, chief!" That sort of thing.

Something else I must tell you about Sunshine; something that makes it such a significant site in the history of working-class politics in Australia. Old H.V., despite his vision of a working-class paradise, was something of a skinflint and underpaid his workers. And the union took him to court in October 1907—the Commonwealth Court of Conciliation and Arbitration, Justice H.B. Higgins presiding. The upshot of the case was that Higgins ruled in favour of the workers, establishing the basic wage in Australia—seven shillings a day, forty-two shillings a week. So, there's Les Twentyman, working-class down to his bootlaces, raised right next door to one of the legendary sites of working-class lore. Anyway, back to old H.V. He recovered from his setback and Sunshine became a model workers' community. And the Sunshine East Primary School, the original school on H.V.'s workers' estate, yep, that was my school. You see what I mean about my working-class pedigree?

So, school's a bit boring for young Les. How does he amuse himself, how does he help the hours pass? By acting up. By making a royal pain in the arse of himself. I spend about half my time at Sunshine East standing in the corridor outside the headmaster's office, waiting to be told off. I was such a regular guest of the headmaster that he got sick and tired of me. "Twentyman, what are you doing here again? Well, I can't be bothered with you. Just stand there and reflect on the wickedness in your skinny frame." On other occasions, he seemed to conceive of me as a kid who might be saved from a lifetime of evil with a few well-chosen words: "Now, Twentyman, you don't really want to take this path to ruin you've chosen, do you? Listen to me young Les, make your parents proud, put your nose to the grindstone, your shoulder to the wheel, pull up your socks, roll up your sleeves, make a legend of yourself amongst schoolboys. Okay?"

"Yes, sir. Of course, sir"

"Back to the classroom, then."

"But sir, the teacher doesn't want me in the classroom. He says I make him contemplate homicide as soon as he lays eyes on me, sir. Bit harsh, wouldn't you say, sir?"

So, what were these infractions of mine that made life so hard for my teachers? Can I even remember? Interruptions, I suppose. Putting my hand up at every opportunity to give absurd answers to questions, such as when we were asked to name the biggest lake in Australia and I said: "Sir! Sir! Jack's Canal, over in Maribyrnong!" Or when we were told to give a definition of a square root: "Sir! Sir! I know the answer but it's a bit embarrassing!" Kids exact a terrible revenge for boredom. But I don't know that I wanted to go down in the annals of Sunshine East Primary as the most difficult kid ever to enter a classroom there. It was just the devil in me. One time we were taking a geography test, knew nothing about geography but I was sitting next to Ian Killip who was enough of a gentleman to let me copy his answers. (His son,

Randal, became a journo, and by a nice twist of fate, helps me out these days with my newspaper column.) Ian came to a question he couldn't answer—'In which state would we find the Blue Mountains?—and he wrote: "I don't know". I looked at his answer, then wrote my own: "Neither do I".

Most of the teachers, I quite liked. One of my tasks these days is to get kids on the street back to school, so you can be sure I wouldn't be telling them about my evil past in the education system. I say: "Oh, the best thing ever was sitting there in class soaking up all that fabulous info".

But I have to tell you, I didn't have it all my own way at Sunshine East. No, no. A couple of kids from the class above me (I was in Grade 4) had decided they didn't like the cut of my jib. Didn't like the look of my face. Didn't like a damned thing about me. What their beef was, I never discovered. Little Les Twentyman, friendliest kid on earth. What's not to like? These two boofheads, they used to wait for me before school, and after. They'd shout out taunts, tell me what they intended to do to me: put me through a mincer and feed me to their dog. I didn't mention that they had a dog with them, the spawn of the devil, grotesque creature with the brain of a retarded wombat. "Yeah, Twentyman, you girl. Gonna flatten you, gonna kick your guts outta ya cakehole!" They scared the hell out of me, I can tell you.

Then one day, a funny thing happened. I was listening to the Boofhead Brothers boasting about the damage they intended to do me and I thought: "You know what, after all this shouting they haven't actually crossed the street and put their plans of murder and dismemberment into action". I thought about what my dad was always telling me: "Don't take rubbish from anyone, son. You don't have to cop rubbish, nonsense." So I thought: "Les, enough is enough". I raced across the street and lit into the both of them. They were, in the time-honoured colloquial expression, as weak as piss. One ran off with a broken nose; the other overtook the first one in the urgency of his retreat. And the dog? Don't recall what I threatened the dog with, but it ran away too. Nice day's work. In the evening, the mother of the boofhead with the broken nose came around full of grievance: "My poor darling boy, a born gentleman, and your boy picked on him and made his nose look like a squashed tomato. Oh, shame on that boy of yours!" My mum knew the story of the boofheads; knew what I'd put up with, and she sent the kid's mother off with a flea in her ear. I'd thought I'd be in all sorts of strife, but when my mum looked at me after the boofhead's mother scuttled away, I knew I needn't have worried. There was tenderness in her look, and maybe also a bit of pride.

Here and there in the west, and elsewhere, I'm looked upon as a bit of tough guy, a warrior, as if my first thought is: "I can settle this thing with a bit of biff and boffo". But no. I've rarely had to raise my dukes, and I don't think I'd enjoy the experience of going a round or two with some of the blokes who've wanted to see my blood hit the sawdust over the years. Some of those blokes truly were tough guys; you could split a length of redgum in half over their heads.

But I stand my ground; I don't back off. And that's given me this reputation as a hard nut, in certain quarters. There are some things you approve of in yourself; other things make you weep with remorse. One of the things I'm glad of in Les Twentyman is that he listened to his dad all those years ago, and made a commitment to scoff at rubbish, scoff at nonsense. I broke the nose of one boofhead; sent another one off holding his skirt up to allow him to muster speed. It's okay by me if I spook certain people these days, without raising a fist. Yeah, I'm happy if they look at me and think: "This bloke, he's serious". I am serious, considering what I'm fighting for. It'd be a damned shame otherwise.

3

Hazards

Every society is haunted by hazards of various sorts. In Syria, one of the big hazards is getting blown to tiny bits by a mortar shell. Survive that, and you have a golden opportunity to starve to death, maybe, or drown in the Aegean or the Adriatic. Big hazards. Here, we're not about to be targeted by a mortar emplacement or a bad guy with an RPG, but we've got some bloody lethal hazards of our own. It's almost as if Satan is saying to us: "Everything sweet in Oz, is it? No landmines, no plague, plenty of big, flash supermarkets? Okay, cop this: methamphetamine; ice." Just to even things up, a taste of hell.

I'm a bit like an ageing professor who's seen thousands of kids go through his institution, thousands, and watched many of them head off to brighter futures than the one they were facing before I met up with them. They remember me. They send me emails, they give me a big gidday if we meet in the streets. "Les! Good to see you, man! Looking as skinny as ever. Not." And they tell me things, often about their own kids. If I ever get a swollen head about this thing or that; feel that I'm leading the poor and the addled to some golden future, a messiah—St. Les of the Bewildered—all I have to do to get back to a more realistic perspective is talk to the people I've helped along in the past. Because their kids are in the same bloody mess that they were, the girls pairing up with the same no-hopers, dodging left hooks and right crosses; the boys thinking: "Oh yeah, oh sure, this is the career for me, knocking over 7-Elevens".

Here and there, a real success, thank Christ; a one-time speed freak who's now the deputy principal of a high school; others who've gone on to run businesses, raise stable families. You know what would be good? This. Once you've got somebody back on the rails, they stay there. For-bloody-ever. Never get visited by the urge to hold their nostrils over ice fumes rising from a glass tube. But that would contradict the foundational rule of my profession: You have to do everything twice. You raise some bloke out of the muck, get him healthy, find him a home. You say: "Well, mate, we're not going to see you again, are we? Except when they tell us you've won the Nobel Peace Prize. Never going to lay hands on a Beretta again, are you? Okay, bye for now." And you know the bloke is going to run around with his Beretta again, threatening somebody or the other. When you see him next time, he's in Remand. "Bloody hell, what did you think you were doing? Another 7-Eleven?" And the bloke says: "Gee, Les, sorry Les, I let you down, mate, but can you speak up for me at the trial?" Twice. Every bloody time. Twice, at least. You've got to be patient in this game.

This is the here and now, 2017. There's a friend of mine, a woman of forty who has a daughter of twenty—a daughter who's been a burden over the years, as you might say. This daughter is in an ice psychosis unit in Dandenong, about to be released. You can't stay in an ice unit forever; the places are needed for other patients. But the mother can't have the daughter in the house; she threw knives at her mum the last time she was at home. The mum, my friend, says: "Les, what's to do, what's to do?" The only thing I can help with is finding a place for the girl in a detox unit, bloody expensive, $34,000 for three months, but around the clock care. I can get the place free. The head of the unit says it's a risk. "The kid's not ready. She's not going to give up ice. Even if she thinks she's ready, I've seen her and I can tell you, she's not." Well, this guy would know. He's seen a lot of ice. So, that's another desperate case that we have to leave in abeyance—wait and see. At any given time, I have maybe fifty of these cases that I need to wait on in my grey matter. This kid, we have to hang on until she's gone past 'desperate' into a place (I have to admit) that I can barely imagine;

somewhere that even she can see is too squalid to be called human. I hate carrying all this degradation around with me, checking every so often to see if Jimmy has been taken away by the paramedics, or if Jenny has finally used up every vein in her body and can no longer get junk into her circulatory system. (Yep, there's still a fair bit of heroin about, mostly for veterans of the syringe who remain loyal to their original poison.)

The truth is this: I'm pretty straight. I've never been interested in hard drugs; I like courtesy; I think people should resist any impulse to rob a 7-Eleven that comes along. And I believe that if you've got kids, take care of them. I'm straighter than my mate, Father Bob, and he's taken vows. I want men and women to behave respectfully to one another; don't go clobbering your missus, and if you find yourself drinking hard spirits straight from the bottle, get help. I like my fellow humans. There it is. So, what I want to know is this: why have I got this creepy bloke stalking me? Is this just one more hazard? Spent my life on the side of the battler, jumped in between blokes with sharpened implements and the innocent parties they were threatening, handed over the last tenner in my wallet to kids who hadn't seen breakfast for a month, and yet I've got this stalker telling people I'm a scoundrel, keeping a journal of my movements, and so on. I'll need to check it out with Father Bob, but maybe even St. Francis had a stalker of his own down there in Assisi, claiming he was a scoundrel, too. But look what I'm doing—putting myself in the company of St. Francis. Get a grip, Les.

My stalker, as it turns out, is nuts. No huge surprise. A minimum qualification for a career as a stalker is that you're nuts. He came around to my street in Braybrook hoping to photograph me emerging from a ritzy mansion in a set of Hugo Boss threads, draped in bling. No such mansions in Braybrook, but there was a house, a little less humble than most, with a Porsche parked in the driveway. He photographed this house and the Porsche and offered a print of the pic to the police as evidence of Les Twentyman living high off the hog. He's also fashioned lists of allegations of one sort and another, suggesting that I'm Australia's Bernie Madoff. The police have conscientiously investigated every allegation. Their conclusion? My stalker is nuts. And while this investigation was going on, my organisation was barred from raising funds for the people we assist, or receiving funds from the government and charities. A whole heap of kids had to go without school books while my stalker's egotism was being looked after. But what the hell can you say? It's unpleasant to be accused of being dishonest, but on the other hand, how often does a simple working-class bloke like me get his own dedicated stalker? Hugh Jackman—well, of course; he might have a dozen. The stalker identifies with his or her target, so they say; a type of union of souls, or at least coverts the target's beauty, that sort of thing. But Les's good looks? Really? No, this bloke, my stalker, once a cop who resigned after a mental breakdown, is an officer of the Department of Human Services, and I've had it suggested that what he truly covets is not my good looks, not my sex appeal, but my reputation. Well, he can't have it, but the next best thing would be to destroy mine. What I want to say to the man is this: mate, if you crave a reputation for something other than being a fool, work for it. I did.

4

Burials

I can remember when ice first came on the street. The drug market has a logic to it, no different from the market for other commodities. A few big shipments of smack find their way to Australia from Myanmar, Northern Thailand, Stan Land (Afghanistan, Tajikistan, Kazakhstan, Turkistan, and so on) and the dealers are faced with an oversupply. Only so much heroin can be absorbed by the addicts of Australia. The price drops as an encouragement to customers to use more; maybe six hits a day instead of four or five; because the dealers have to keep the stuff moving. They can't say to their suppliers: "Don't need any next month". They're locked into a deal that provides them with junk at spaced intervals. They can't afford to have a big shed out on

Donnybrook Road full of unsold merchandise. With junk, it's got to be here today, gone tomorrow. When the stuff's in short supply, same logic, except the price goes up and unscrupulous operators (shocking, I know, but there are a few about in the junk business) mix what they sell with all sorts of muck. Some of these cheap adulterants are worse for you than the drug. Yep, the price goes up and addicts who were getting used to six sessions a day are struggling to pay for the basic four. And in that situation, every DVD player in town is in jeopardy: in through the window, out the back door, over the fence—twenty seconds. The skills of rapid entry and departure some of these kids possess would do credit to a commando.

Now, heroin is the granddaddy of the drug trade. We've had it in Australia for a hundred years. Everything that heroin can do to your system, we know about. I see a kid in dreamland behind a skip and I know it's smack. Or I see a kid fidgeting and scratching and constantly running his hand through his hair, her hair, and I know what it is: hanging out for good old smack. Speed, yeah, I know what I'm dealing with, lots of giggling, crazy optimism, it's speed. Ice, when it came along in the 1990s, this was different. You don't usually go berserk when smack's your drug of choice—sometimes, but it's uncommon. Ice users, bloody hell, paranoid delusions, about ten times their normal strength, they can run a knife into someone's guts without knowing what they're doing. A true bastard of a drug. When I first saw kids on ice, all I could think was:

dear God, what evil genius invented this? It's the purest of the methamphetamines. Enough hike in it to put you into orbit. Cops, paramedics, they hate it. Turn up to where some kid's raving about zombies and little green men and get whacked over the head with half a house brick. And it's bad for the bowels, ice; the paramedics have to deal with full trousers now and again. Ice took over as the drug-of-choice of the junk connoisseurs.

The worse thing for people in outreach like me was seeing kids in the care of ice addicts. With smack, there's a bit of hope that mum or dad will plonk a bowl of Weetbix down in front of the kids every so often, maybe fry a chop, tall glass of a health beverage like Fanta or Coke. But if the parents have got their heads in glass tubes full of fumes, the kids are buggered. Mum and dad, they're not human anymore; they're more likely to strangle you than feed you. I never feel like treating any of the addicts I come across as if they were sinners. They can see in the occasional lucid moment that they've fucked up. They know, most of them, that they've got to find some way of getting off the gear. But here's the thing. Smack, ice, speed, coke—they have a greater attraction to anyone who's tried them than other sources of pleasure. Sex, booze, beautiful food, love—nothing comes close.

The high you get out of the gear, it must be bloody, bloody hard to give up. Bloody hard. We're talking about various forms of paradise. Nobody wants to give that up. I've looked into the eyes of young men, young women as they swear to me that they're going clean. They believe it for the moment. But listen, once the gear is your life, there's nothing else. The only people you can get along with are those who are on the gear themselves. The only people who understand you. The only people you can talk to. The only people you don't have to apologise to, mumble out some sort of rationalisation. There's the world, and then there's gear. You can't have both. Whatever beauty and consolation other people find in life, it's lost to you. I can tell you, it's a fucking tragedy because no matter what an addict believes, the gear is not the world. You have to find your joy in the smiles of your kids or there's no hope for you. The gear will squeeze everything out of you, even the thrill of scoring, in the end. I've known addicts who no longer even get the buzz out of heroin, ice, coke that they once did. It's winner takes everything, and the junk is always the winner.

I get into a sad sort of state whenever I speak about junk. Tears, anger. It probably shows even here on the page. You have to make allowances for me. I've been to so many burials of kids who've overdosed or curled up in the corner of a car park and succumbed to any of a dozen afflictions resulting from drug use. Untreated gashes that have become septic, for example. People on junk are always falling over, same as drunks, and they're too stoned to break the fall, too stoned to feel the pain, lose a litre of blood without even noticing. Untreated Hep C is another cause, liver failure, bloody awful. Malnutrition. Kids on junk get warnings from health workers, paramedics, doctors in clinics: "Hey, man, eat something". So, the kid goes to Woolies in Smith Street or Acland Street, steals a tin of Sustagen, gets through it in an hour: "Okay, don't need to eat for a week". You can die of malnutrition on Sustagen, but the poor kid doesn't know that.

At the burials I attend, there are never more than three or four people at the graveside. Hardly ever a service in a chapel; just the burial. Me, the gravedigger, one of two undertakers contracted by the state to oversee paupers' interments. Never so much as a bunch of flowers, unless I bring them. It's a bloody harrowing business, burying a kid so lost to his or her mum and dad that they don't even know this daughter or son of theirs is dead. I hardly ever have any details that would allow me to track down a father, a mother. It's just some kid I know as 'Jamie' or 'Melissa'; some kid I've been called to take a look at down at the cop shop, in hospital, in an alley. The next time I'm contacted it's a cop telling me that the kid I saw in Hosiers Lane a few weeks ago, is now in the morgue. If I glance about, I can see other graves that I've stood beside, all of them unmarked by a headstone or a cross, just earth gradually subsiding, blades of couch grass taking root in the clay. Sometimes it's raining and I'll be standing there under an umbrella, brushing tears away with the back of my hand. How can I not cry? Christ, it's a lonely death for these kids.

The undertakers might ask me if I want to say a few words. I shake my head. I couldn't keep this kid alive, nobody could, so what would I say? At these times of burial, I nearly always think of Libby, a girl I knew back in the early '80s when I worked in a Carlton hostel. She'd been in state care for years, but was released to fend for herself at the age of sixteen. Fend for herself? What chance did she have? She'd never built up a relationship of trust with anyone, and she had no map of the future in her head—you know, finish school, apply for uni or Tafe, find some part-time job while she's studying, meet a boy she liked, that sort of thing. None of these kids have a map. It's just today, and to hell with tomorrow. Or maybe it's wrong to say that addicts have no map of the future. They do. But the maps are limited in the terrain they cover—they show where the kids stand, where their dealer can be found, and the shortest route between the two points. This was at a time when AIDS was scaring the shit out of everyone, and anyone on junk could be pretty sure that if the smack didn't kill them, the virus would. But Libby and I became friends. I argued with her, tried to steer her into rehab, with limited success. I told her she'd be dead in two years unless she listened to me. But really, telling anyone on smack that the future is the graveyard, just gets you an indifferent look and a bland reply: "Yeah, yeah, you're probably right".

Here's an example of Libby's comic touch. I had to go looking for her once in the back streets of St Kilda, can't recall the specific need I had to contact her. Wandered down Jackson Street that runs behind the shops on Fitzroy Street, then Burnett Street, Dalgety Lane, Robe Street. This part of West St Kilda is the favoured worksite of girls on the game, has been for decades. Libby was on the game, naturally—about sixteen. I found her and was engaged in a chat, probably to do with getting her back in the Canning Street hostel, when a car pulled up. A bloke rolled down the driver's side window. "Hey, love," he called. "How about coming back to my place for a cup of coffee and a fuck?" Libby broke off the conversation with me to reply to this boofhead: "I don't drink coffee!" Had to smile.

The thing I loved in Libby was her zest for life. Now, everything I've said about addicts might make this sound crazy because junk builds a wall between the addict and the world. But there you go. Full of life, fabulous sense of humour. The sort of advice you get from people experienced in the drug scene, people who do whatever they can to help kids like Libby, is never to allow yourself to be drawn too close; never invest your hope for these kids too deeply, because they're going to break your heart. The kids don't want to break your heart, but the junk is a tyrant and they'll have no choice. Good advice; pity it's never been possible for me to benefit from it. I draw too close all the time. I want the kids to survive, maybe reach a point at which they can become functioning addicts, hold down a job even while they continue to use. This can happen, especially with heroin. If an addict survives till thirty, he or she has a reasonable chance of making it to forty. Junkies pick up skills over the years. They get savvy enough to avoid overdosing. They know the strength of what they're using just from a taste on the tongue, or sometimes just by looking at the stuff. They learn to inject out of harm's way—by which I mean, not in the middle of the Bourke Street Mall, where they're likely to blunder into the path of a 96 tram. They teach themselves to sometimes eat food that actually has a little bit of nutritional value. They don't try to scale three-metre-high back fences with a stolen laptop tucked under their arm. They become veterans of addiction—a phrase I've used before. And that's one of the few skinny little hopes you've got, and that I had for Libby—that I could get her out of enough fucked-up situations with dealers and whatever to see her through to the veteran class. (I have to tell you, Libby repaid my dedication. She saved my life one time when it looked like curtains for Les.)

I lost contact with Libby when I went to work down in Sunshine. When I next heard her mentioned it was to be told that she'd died a while ago. And what was it that killed her? A heroin overdose. I asked the question but I didn't need to. The guy who gave me this unwelcome news didn't know where she was buried. I made enquiries, but no deal. You know what they tell actors in a role that calls for them to cry at a certain stage in the drama? "Think of someone you loved who's gone to God." Well, if I were that actor, I'd only have to think of Libby and her smile, her laughter, her joy. And I'd also think of her grave, because I did finally get the information I'd been chasing for eight years. She was buried in Bulla Cemetery.

I drove out along the Tullamarine Freeway past the airport to Sunbury Road, down Oaklands Road—a pretty barren area, flat and windy. The Bulla Cemetery sits just across the way from the Dog Exhibition Centre, God knows what that is. I left my car in Uniting Lane and walked into the cemetery and with the help from the cemetery keepers found Libby's numbered grave. The mound of earth that sits above all new graves had subsided in the years since her burial. Christ, it was a desolate sight. This quicksilver girl, so ready to laugh, sometimes at me, and this was the last of her; a numbered grave in a windswept graveyard, the very earth that covered her trampled by kids taking a shortcut to school through the headstones. I stood over her grave with tears picking a path through my stubble. I don't spend much time thinking about death and all that mysterioso stuff, an afterlife and so on, but I spend a lot of time thinking about lives like Libby's.

When I left the graveside, I met up with the cemetery keepers again. They could see I was in a bad way. One of them told me that Libby's wasn't the only unmarked grave in the cemetery. Forty-eight all up, many of them one-time wards of the state, a fair number whose bodies had never been claimed by family members or friends, as if they were no more than debris. The main two causes of death of these kids were overdose and suicide.

I can tell you this for free: if you've got kids and think that issues around drug use concern people on the other side of town, think again. I've known kids from very fancy suburbs who ended up giving hand-jobs in car parks to get junk. I feel as much sorrow for those kids as I do for wards of the state—the unwanted, the abandoned. But Libby—she was special.

"Don't get too close to them, Les. They'll break your heart. Step back."

Bloody oath, they'll break your heart.

5

Jobseeker

I had the good fortune to be a teenager in the 1960s, and you could probably say that about every kid of my age in the western world. The music, the feeling you got of things freeing up, more candour about sex. All good. Even though Australia was in the midst of a credit squeeze in the early years of the decade and lots of people were doing it tough, I can still sincerely say that you were better off as a teenager in the '60s than at any time since forever. Because after the credit squeeze there were jobs galore, plus the music, plus the sex. A kid like me, out of high school after four years, no problem, went straight into employment with Vic Railways. This was 1963. I turned up to apply for the job of assistant clerk, they gave me a few sums to do, I thought: "Piece of cake". And so it was. I was good at arithmetic. It was playing footy that sharpened my wits, keeping track of the score all through the game, nutting out our percentage and so on. Yep, good brain for figures and the railway people said: "Les, you're a genius with numbers, we've got a job for you in the pay office. Here's your uniform, here's your weapon, here's your holster." They handed me a Browning .44, five rounds, told me not to shoot anyone unnecessarily, put me in the care of another bloke somewhat older, gave us a bag packed with thick wads of notes and sent us out to the various sites where railway people were employed. In those days, people were paid in cash—no cheques, no direct debit, just good old folding money. "Suits me," I thought. I felt like the sheriff in a Western.

Off we hiked with our big bag of dough down through the city. We were on our way to an office of the railways situated in Lonsdale Street, behind the Myer Emporium. My mate says to me: "Might take a shortcut through the store, what do you think?" Les, with all the wisdom of a sixteen-year-old working-class kid from the tough suburbs, says: "Yep!" Passing the escalator that went up from the ground floor to the first, my gun fell out of the holster. Must have knocked it with my hand, or something. Fell on the metal escalator step with a clatter. Crowds of people around. Some bloke, a genuine willy wet-leg, went into hysterics and shouted: "A gun! It's a hold-up!" I said: "It's not a hold-up, moron. I just dropped my gun". This set off another flock of shoppers: "Oh God, a gun! We'll all be killed, save me, save me!" I probably shouldn't have held it against them that they were such weaklings since they were only hoping to pass the day in Myers without getting shot through the head, but I did. Meanwhile, my Browning was going up the escalator unattended. I leapt up the steps two at a time and overtook the weapon before it reached the first floor. Me and my offsider hurried away. These days, I would have been locked up in the Russell Street nick, become the subject of an enquiry by a panel of judges, while everyone who saw the gun or knew someone who saw the gun would have entered six months of trauma counselling.

Now, you'd need very limited ambition to settle into carrying canvas bags hither and yon for the rest of your life. It wasn't long before I started to moan softly to myself: "There must be more to life than this". I had before me at the office the perfect example of what I did not want to become—a senior clerk by the name of Phillip who kept to his desk from 9 o'clock in the morning to midday, moving pieces of paper from Pile A to Pile B. He glanced up at the clock every thirty seconds, and at 12 o'clock exactly he'd hoist himself to his feet in his fawn cardigan, and shuffle off to a pub up the road in North Melbourne; three or four beers for lunch, shuffle back to the office, fall asleep at his desk for the rest of afternoon. I'd gaze at him with his head on the desk, snoozing away, mouth slightly open, and think: "If that's me in five years, I'll kill myself".

A woman who worked in the branch—the only woman in the place—must have noticed me gazing in fear and disgust at the comatose figure of Phil snoring at his desk, because she took me aside and gave me the benefit of her wisdom. Kath Green was her name, and she'd been at the branch for thirty years. Christ knows how, but she still had a functioning heart and soul after all that time. She said: "Les, you don't want to be doing this all your life. Just take a look around the place. These blokes, they've got no life. Nothing happening in their grey matter. Listen to me. There's real life in you, pet. Don't throw it away in this place." You see, it's not enough to know that routine is bound to grind you down, rob you of initiative. Often you need someone else to tell you. Kath, she didn't want to see any man turn into a vegetable but she chose me to talk to because for most of the others, all hope was lost. "You're clever," she said. "Keep an eye out. Look in the papers. Lots of jobs in the papers. Try things that you haven't even thought about. Don't wither away here, Les." There's a message here about purpose, isn't there? At times in the past, any job would do. In the depression of the late 1920s and early 1930s, men were lining up for the chance to work for sixpence an hour digging turnips. And if they got the job, they rejoiced. In times like that, nobody thought of employment that did something for your soul. The sad truth is your belly comes before your soul. But your belly doesn't have the final say all the time. I wanted what we now call fulfilment, and I took Kath's words to heart.

Not immediately. For the time being, I thought: "Les, keep this mug of a job, get a second one to go with it, make some dough, then get into something you can enjoy". I found a second job. Oh, boy. Pouring liquid concrete into moulds at a factory in Braybrook. Bloody hell. Hard yakka; the hardest of yakka I've ever experienced, in fact. Hot, dirty, physically exhausting, like serving time in a quarry with a prison gang. Finished at the railways at four in the arvo; started work at the Braybrook factory at five and slaved away until one in the morning. The only way I could cope was to tell myself that many people worked even harder. "It's not the Burma Railway, Les. You're not on the pick and shovel at Hellfire Pass. Could be worse. Possibly." At the same time as I was holding down those two jobs, I was playing footy for the Willy Under 19s. And as fate would have it, one day I broke my leg. We played in the mud back then, or better to say that the rain that made the ovals into swamps, didn't drain away; no such thing as fancy subterranean piping. There I am, stretched out in the muck, broken leg, and I'm thinking: "Thank you, God! I don't have to go back to that mongrel of a factory."

It's one thing to know that you're not enjoying the job you've got, and it's another to find a job you *can* enjoy. It took me years to grasp exactly what I was good at, what I could give myself to and reap some satisfaction. So what was I good at? Sport. And to be good at sport, I had to keep fit. So I was good at sport and keeping fit. Just as this dawned on me, about 1970, 1971, I met Brendan Edwards. That was either ordinary good luck, or an example of my stars aligning. Brendan had been a star in the centre for the

Hawthorn footy club in the VFl, fabulous overhead mark, extremely agile, became known as Twinkle Toes. But even a champion like Brendan couldn't make a full living out of footy. The coach of a team would say to a player the team wanted to keep: "I'll tell you what, lad, we'll give you twenty quid a game and throw in a leg of lamb each week, maybe a dozen snags, too, and a couple of packets of Rothmans. Best deal I can offer." Footy players had to have a job away from the game. Some were plumbers, like Ian Mort at Hawthorn, some were labourers, some were used car salesmen. Brendan, he had more savvy than most and he started up a gym, then another, then another. He got into the business at a time when a visit to the gym was becoming a more accepted part of people's lives, and he thrived.

Can't recall the circumstances of my meeting up with Brendan, but it would have something to do with footy, you'd think. Anyway, he saw in me a bloke with some potential and he asked me to take a job at his Sunshine gym. Man, I loved it. This was something I could imagine enjoying for the rest of my life. You know how it feels when what you're good at becomes your livelihood. Got savvy with all the equipment, knew the routines, found pleasure in helping people master the programs. Each morning I was in charge of big classes of women, demanding stuff because we're not talking about a bit of a jig in time to a disco tune, no way; these women were serious—trampolines, stationary bikes, pumping iron. This was a time—the start of the '70s—when middle-class women were looking to get the hell out of the kitchen and grab hold of a bigger life. Lifting 100 Ks above their heads wasn't butch any longer—it was mainstream. It gave me real pleasure to see these women thrive, driven on by new ambitions.

I must mention a strange episode that occurred, not at the gym, but just across the road at a supermarket. I was outside the gym for some reason, smoking a Cuban cigar, eating an éclair, can't remember, but I was there on the footpath when a woman came shuffling out of the supermarket and sat down on a low brick fence that ran along the footpath. She seemed to me to be in distress, bent over, one hand on her chest. I put aside my cigar or jam bun and hurried over to her, asked her if she was okay. "Can't get my breath," she said. "Something's wrong." She was young, maybe in her mid-twenties, no obvious reason for her to be suffering in the way she was. My car was parked just out the front of the gym, so I helped her on board and whizzed her down to a nearby GP. A couple of days passed before I phoned up the GP and asked how the woman had fared. He said: "Put her in hospital. She died, Les. Her ticker." I thought: "Oh fuckin' hell!" I was upset, more than was warranted by the death of a woman who was a stranger to me. A day or so later, a bloke came into the gym, asked for me (must have been given my name by the doc) and thanked me for the help I'd given his wife. He thought that she might have survived if someone had noticed her condition earlier. After that, I was especially watchful with the women in my classes. Any of them felt a little dizzy, I was in there like a shot. "How long have you had these symptoms?" "Symptoms of what, Les? Calm down."

Well, then, I'm in the right game, getting along beautifully when one fine day Brendan asked me if I'd like to buy his share of the Sunshine gym. He wanted to diversify, try his hand at other things. I said: "You bet". The asking price was more than I could afford, so I brought in my mate David Thorpe, who coached with me at Yarraville Footy Club. (Don't ask me to name all the footy clubs I've coached. About ten thousand.) We emptied our pockets, bought the gym and set about making a motza, as we hoped. Except that we didn't make much at all. What was the problem? Dunno. Not that brilliant at making dough. David, same as me—not a genius with capital. Also, many more gyms were starting up, a lot of competition. David and I, we were the next thing to bankrupt, owed dough everywhere, even to the lolly man who stocked the snack bar. Bloody depressing. I said to myself: "Les, you're never going to have a bank account with more in it than a zack and a couple of old pennies". I'd been hoping to make enough to buy my own house, not a pie-in-the-sky hope, really, but even the deposit on a two-bedroom fibro at the back of Braybrook was beyond me. David fared even worse than me. He lost his house. Our accountant, Tony Cerantonio, came up with the idea of me asking my mum and dad to cover the debts of the gym. I said no, categorically no. I mean, bloody hell? My parents had worked hard all their lives for what they had. I wasn't about to pour their life savings into my business. I was in my mid-twenties, not a kid. If you make a mess, clean it up yourself.

There's a sort of cosmic thing known as the law of divine compensation and it says that the Universe or God or whatever throws you a bit of good fortune to make up for the bloody awful mess you might have made of things. Like saying: "Les, mate, never seen such an arse-about way of going about things. But look closely and you'll find a little nugget in the muck." That little nugget was the goodwill the gym had developed with the schools of the region over the years. No government school had a gym of its own back then, so the Phys Ed staff of the local schools used to bring the kids to our Sunshine gym. And at this very time of my desolation, St. Paul's in Altona was looking for a Phys Ed teacher. St. Paul's was a Catholic school, but the headmaster there, Father Winters, had heard of me and, after a recommendation from Brother Bouchard from Chisholm College in Braybrook, was prepared to give me a job as a sports master. Brendan had encouraged me to study for a qualification back in the days of my first employment at the Sunshine gym, so I was in a position to satisfy St. Paul's on that score.

We'd had the St. Paul's kids at the gym a few times, with Father Winters accompanying them. When he spoke to me about the position at the school, he said he was particularly taken with the way I motivated the kids. He also commended me on the way I kept 'a safe distance between myself and the kids'. He meant that there was no risk of me buttering up the kiddies for extra-curricular stuff. In our day and age, we pretty much regard Catholic schools of the past—and not that far past—as havens for paedophiles; and no doubt Father Winters had seen evidence here and there of the brothers—some of them—salivating over the boys in the showers; so he was pleased that he didn't have to worry about me going ga-ga in the nooks and crannies of the school.

Four years at St. Paul's. Good years. Regular income, fulfilling work. But I had to battle the school hierarchy over the status of sport in the curriculum. Those in charge understood that sport and exercise had to be part of the broad program, but they thought it a trivial part. Scholastic excellence meant much more to them than excellence on the playing field. I argued that sport should be given the same status as any other subject. I recall telling the brothers at one review of the Phys Ed department: "Look, we need our Macfarlane Burnets, but we need our Bradmans, too. Absolutely. They deserve to be revered for their different achievements." Nicely put, don't you think? Could have been a speechwriter.

But it was a job that had its downside, I must admit. Such a hassle getting the kids to the swimming pool, to the gym, what have you. The school had a few vehicles used for transporting the kids about but the people in charge wouldn't give them to me. To get the kids to Mass—oh, sure! And I complained. There it is, out in the open—I complained.

I've complained all my life. It's me, Les, the complainer, the mouth, the fella who won't shut up. Not on my own behalf, for someone else who can't do it for himself, herself. It's as much a part of me as my face. In my private life, I'm a pussycat. Give me a pat and I purr. But for a cause that means something, nope, I just can't keep my gob shut. And that's okay, isn't it? The country may not need a thousand Les Twentymans, or even ten, or even two. But one, yeah, we definitely need one.

So I'm saying to the brothers: "Gotta get the kids to the pool. We need a bus." And the brothers say: "Oh, no, Les, no no no. The bus is reserved for the special Mass on the third Tuesday after the first Wednesday on the fifth Sunday after Lent." And Les, who should know better, says: "Now listen here, Brother Bob, it's all very well nourishing the souls of the boys, but they'd be a damned sight better off swimming freestyle laps and practising tumble turns". Another thing that annoyed me was the horrible quality of the fare that the school allowed to be served in the tuckshop. I wrote a piece for the school newsletter, a masterpiece of erudite prose in which I described the kids as 'human dustbins'. The local paper, the *Footscray Mail* somehow got sight of the piece and reprinted it, full page, with a cartoon. That excited the interest of that noble rag, the *Truth*, a newspaper that specialised in the sensational. You know how it works, someone in government advocates more education in schools about drug use and the *Truth*'s headline is: 'Minister Wants Heroin in Kindergartens'. A journo from the *Truth* rings me up and says: "Les, what's all this about crap food in school canteens? Want to say more about that?" Do I want to say more? Does Les Twentyman want to say more? What do you think! I told him of a doctor I'd spoken to with a surgery next to a girls' boarding school who claimed that the students ate such horrible food that a few of the older girls who'd fallen pregnant (one way or another) and had come to the surgery had subsequently suffered miscarriages due to lousy nutrition. It was a story with very dubious evidence to support it, sure, but *Truth* journos considered evidence a mere nuisance. The headline for the story was: 'Schoolgirls Who Eat Pies Don't Need the Pill!' When the edition came out, I was called up to the headmaster's office: "Les, what the bloody hell is this? Pies? The pill? Are you completely insane?" And me: "Just trying to make a point, Brother Pete". My mum saw the story, too. She was mortified, being a bit of a Christian; saw it as an attack on everything holy on earth and wouldn't say a word to me for a month.

So, St. Paul's and Les were no longer such close friends. The embedded prejudices of the Catholic way of looking at things began to clash more and more often with the embedded prejudices of the Twentyman way of looking at things. And this was simmering away in my guts when one of the brothers called me aside for what he said would be, "a word to the wise". He asked me if was true that I was living in a de facto relationship with 'a woman' (as he termed it). I said: "Yeah, I'm living with Margaret Rutherford. What's it to you?" (I may have been a bit politer at the time, but not much.) The brother said: "Les, my boy, in the eyes of the God of the Catholic Church it is a sin, a black, heinous sin to live with a woman or even to enjoy a roll in the hay with a woman to whom you are not married. I'm sorry, Les, but there it is. Comes straight from Jesus who blessed the union of husband and wife in the marriage at Cana, where he turned water into wine. You have to marry Miss Rutherford if you are to continue in your position at St. Paul's." Or words to that effect. I was stunned. Bloody Hell! Other staff members were living in de facto relationships and nothing had been said to them. I think the hierarchy of the school had decided that I had to go. Once again, it was my mouth that had landed me in trouble. But there's good trouble and bad trouble. And this was good trouble, trouble worth risking.

All the same, Margaret and I married. Okay, it could have been a bit sooner than we'd intended, but we were going to marry anyway. We laid on water for the reception in demijohns and I personally turned it into shiraz and champagne. Nothing to it. And what do you know?— St. Paul's and I said fare-thee-well to each other at the end of the year.

One door slams shut, another door swings open. I was in the good books with Sister Giovanni of Mount St. Joseph's Girls School over in Altona West after helping out with the school's attempt on the netball world record. One of the lesser known world records, I agree, but Mount St. Joseph's landed it by playing netball for fifty-two hours without a break. It was a little bit nuts, but the girls were into it and I was courtside shouting encouragement and clapping and whistling. "Yay girls, go! Flip that ball! Hurrah and hosanna!" The girls would have kept it up and set a record that would last for eternity, but they had to go Mass. So, there you go. Satisfied the Guinness Book of Records, and satisfied Jesus. All good.

Sister Giovanni gave me a job to begin at the start of Term 1 in 1976. Smooth changeover from the 800 boys of St. Paul's to the 800 girls of Mount St. Joseph's. Same deal—Phys Ed, sport. The school was almost entirely staffed by women—me and one or two other blokes and that was the whole male complement. An emphatically female environment. It was terrific. I've always got along well with women. Never plagued by sexist phobias. And the nuns were especially kind to me because, as a non-Catholic, there was a chance to save my soul, maybe help me see the light. They didn't come after me with dogma; they mothered me.

Five years at Mount St. Joseph's. Happy years. My marriage to Margaret came to an end during that time, a low point, but otherwise, happy as a lark. Great respect for Sister Giovanni. Intelligent, subtle, a huge heart. The sort of woman who found her true calling when she took the veil. Also, a good sense of humour, I must say. Sister Gionanni, if you're reading this, you'll remember the time all those brand new softballs were nicked from the PE storeroom?

Searched high and low, couldn't find them, finally and with failing patience I went looking for you and found you with a classroom full of Year 10 girls. "Excuse me, Sister," I said, "have you or any of the girls seen my softballs? Brand new they were, can't find 'em anywhere." Well, Year 10 girls. What was I thinking? Every single one of them produced a purpose-designed snigger. And Sister G, I assert before God, I got a snigger out of you, too.

But, you know, ambition. Bloody hell. The time came when I desperately needed to be my own boss again, return to running a gym. I said goodbye to Sister Giovanni and all the staff at Mount St. Joseph's and took on the running of a gym at the Highpoint Shopping Centre in Maribyrnong in partnership with a mate, John Evans. Now, what I might have said to myself was this: "Les, mate, you had a crack at running a gym and it cost you every zack in the till. Don't do it again, pal. Don't bankrupt yourself doing something you haven't got the savvy for. The money side of it, Les. It's not for you. Don't do it."

I did it. Went broke. Kelvin Templeton and Terry Wheeler from the Bullies—the Footscray Football Club—took over the complex from us. I settled into a stint of unemployment. Bloody depressing. I was coaching the Yarraville Football Club for two thousand bucks a season, but you can't live on that. My car was repossessed. I swapped a cricket bat signed by the entire Pakistani team for a coat. I thought: "Les, it's come to this. You haven't got enough dough to clothe yourself. You're a sorry spectacle."

The Catholics came to my rescue, once again. Maybe the nuns who'd mothered me at Mount St. Joseph's snuck in a special prayer for Les at morning Mass. "Dear God, do something for Les Twentyman. He's in strife. Good bloke, good heart, but tries to run businesses and gets it all arse-side-up. Find a job for him in a nice Catholic school, Father, if you can, over and out and amen." St. Joseph's Catholic Primary in Collingwood offered me a part-time job teaching Phys Ed for a few months. I made enough for a pie and chips every so often, but not much more.

Making enough to live on is a task that goes on all your life, for many. The whole idea of finding a job that you can enjoy day after day—it's a bit of a fantasy. What happens, for most people, is that they struggle along, sometimes satisfied, sometimes discontented, try their hand at this, at that, then one fine day they make a breakthrough. Or, like me, you make the breakthrough, get a bee in your bonnet, leave your job to make a mint running a business, discover your incompetence, and begin the struggle all over again. It's life.

But there was something up ahead for me, as a matter of fact. Before I reached it, I put in time selling used cars for a mate of mine from Braybrook, Mike Good. He kept a yard in Elwood. I was there for eight months and spent just about the whole of that time holding lengthy conversations with prospective customers about footy, politics, what have you, only rarely touching on fuel consumption and hire purchase arrangements, the old drip-feed. Not so many visits to the till to ring up a sale. None. Had to concede that I probably wasn't cut out to be a used car salesman. Don't know that it would mean anything good about me if I was. Mike, sure. Top bloke. Les?—no.

Okay, eight months in the car yard, then I got word about a job I'd applied for in a girls' hostel in Carlton. And what business did I have applying for a job in a girls' hostel in Carlton or anywhere? Zero qualifications, unless you wanted to look at my experience teaching girls how to run and jump and play netball. The advertisement asked for someone who was willing to work with 'difficult female adolescents'. I thought, well, I've had a little bit of that, girls in the classes I've taught getting aggro, "Hey Les, Mandy won't let me use the weights, the fucker, I'm going to smash her stupid face in for her!" But maybe not on a daily basis. And maybe not with girls who carry knives, and know how to use them. Still, how hard can it be, Les?

6

Hostel

How hard can it be? Very, bloody hard, that's what! These were girls who came from backgrounds of horrifying abuse, now wards of the state; taken away from their parents for their own good, the abuse having been perpetrated at home. Okay, there was a lot for me to get my brain around, but as a matter of fact, I had a natural sympathy for these kids and something like an instinctive understanding of what was going on in their heads and hearts. That understanding wasn't based on personal experience; my mum and dad were models of loving concern. But it was there in my head, that compassion for the battler, for the victim.

The hostel was up in Canning Street, a two-storey Victorian terrace, very fancy building, high wall along the front and down the side. A maximum of six girls at a time. And, oh God, those six girls had packed into their lives more mischief than any six hundred girls outside. Most of them, and I'm talking about girls of fourteen, had been on the game. There were a couple of brothels not far from the hostel; the girls had seen the inside of them. A big problem was the pimps. In their line of work, a hostel that kept the girls away from the customers was a disaster, a restraint of trade. And it could happen that the pimps would see me as the do-gooder who'd put himself in the path of profit. A pimp's weapon of choice is the blade, rather than the pistol. A blade gives you more options than a firearm. You might want to let a bit of blood flow without actually killing your girl, engage in a certain amount of torture as you lay down the law. The pimps would produce their blades to threaten me, such as the time I spoke of earlier when Libby had to intervene to save my bacon.

Now this job in the hostel, it was special. I don't want to sound as if I've got tickets on myself, but with this job I'd found my vocation. There's a theory that every human being is born with an encoded vocation, and that your whole life is an attempt to discover it. Some people never find it, but those who do, know it when it happens. Of course, not all vocations are wholesome. The vocation of some is serial murder, or cracking safes, or being in every way possible a bloody nuisance. But this was my vocation, connecting with kids, and I could feel the certainty of it in my heart and my guts.

The job wasn't complex; nothing like that. Just demanding. We taught the kids life skills, and bloody hell, they needed them. You see, this is what you miss out on if you're raised in a household with a dad who's melting cubes of hash on the kitchen stove to sell in baggies, and a mum who's turning tricks with unsavoury strangers in the bedroom. Never a time when your mum says: "Come here, darling, I'm going to teach you how to make ratatouille". Or when your dad says: "I'll drive, you use the Melways and navigate". Personal hygiene—no tutorials. How to prepare yourself for a job interview—nothing. Shopping to a budget in the supermarket (as opposed to shoplifting)—never happens. Even such a simple task as making your bed—no instruction. And none of the helpful nagging of a mum and dad. "Melanie, have you cleaned your teeth? Did you clean them properly? Top teeth, ninety seconds, bottom teeth, ninety seconds."

Growing up is a group effort, lots of input from parents; but the girls in the hostel had none of that. You have to want to please your mum and dad at a certain level. You have to value being told: "Good girl, good job". If your dad is having sex with you, you don't have a vestige of respect for him. If your mum's handing you over to some salivating cretin for the price of a whack of smack, no, you don't want to listen to a damned thing she says. You've just got yourself, and your sorrow.

The girls were always on edge, always overwrought. Well, naturally. Some were strung out after four days without smack. Some hadn't had more than a couple of hours of sleep a night for a week, things going around and around in their heads. The girls never had the chance to enjoy normal, calm, down-time, chill time. Remember what I said about not having a map of the future? They thought they'd be dead before any sort of a future could unfold. Listen to this episode in the kitchen: Libby (the girl I spoke about, sometimes the best company in the world with her wit and humour, sometimes not) was preparing dinner (life skills), cutting up the vegetables that another girl, Clare, had brought back from the supermarket. I'm there watching, because you can never leave the girls unsupervised with sharpened implements; homicide is always on their minds, or suicide. So, Libby's swinging a big, sharp stainless steel cleaver at the chopping board, while Clare's stuffing everything into a big pot. Suddenly Libby stops, looks left and right.

"Where're the sprouts?"

"Sprouts?" says Clare.

"Yeah, the sprouts, Brussels sprouts. I told you to get a dozen sprouts. Where are they?'

Clare mumbles something, and I'm all at once alert and watchful.

"What'd you say?"

"I said, I forgot them."

"You forgot them? How could you forget them, moron? You had a list!"

"Yeah, well I did. So, shut your face, you fucking moll."

Ah, yes. Right there—trouble. I was already lunging to get myself between Libby and Clare, just as the raised cleaver comes down. Didn't quite manage to part Clare's skull down the middle, but came damned close. I'm shouting for calm, Libby's trying to make a second attempt at murder, Clare runs out the front door.

It took hours to pacify Libby. The girls had no experience of restraint. They had never witnessed it in their parents, never seen the benefit of holding back, exercising self-control. I said to Libby: "Okay, let's say you'd managed to brain Clare with the cleaver. Killed her stone dead. You know what comes next? A murder trial. The Crown versus Libby. They'd put me in the witness box, and the barrister for the Crown, he'd say, 'Mr Twentyman, tell us in your own words about the events leading up to this brutal murder of poor dead Clare'. And I'd have to say: 'The brussels sprouts. Clare forgot to buy the sprouts at Woolies, and so Libby gave her a whack with the cleaver.' And the judge says: 'Mr Twentyman, are you suggesting that this murder was all over a Brussel sprout or two? Don't tell me!' Is that what you want, Lib? Life behind bars because of a bloody Brussel sprout?" Libby did see the comedy in it.

The hostel could never be a home for the girls. They didn't know what a 'home' was, sure, but somehow or other they each had an idea of what 'home' might be—probably no more than a place of complete safety, of plenty, a full refrigerator, warmth, a pussycat to stroke, a telly that works; no mother or father to make their lives a misery. They treated the hostel as a facility. A month on the streets or in the brothel, a month of four whacks of smack a day, a month of despair and they'd come back to the hostel for a few days, shower, get some proper food into their system, enjoy time away from their pimps, slaps across the chops, a blade held against their throats. But then the more persistent features of their lives would return, not just the hunger for gear but something else much weirder: the hunger for the street, for danger, even for their pimps. It might seem perverse, but out on the streets, many of the girls experienced the only power they had ever known; the only mastery. They knew the streets. They knew all the tricks of the trade. They knew how to make a man tremble with lust. And when they met up with their dealers, they could pull $150 out of their pockets and hand it over, and take possession of that baggie of smack. They'd made the money, they'd made the purchase. In an arse-about way, that was power.

No girl in the hostel had less appetite for extended stays than Fiona. Never gave the slightest trouble while she was in the hostel; no fights, no abuse, quiet as a mouse. But when she'd had her fill of the place—that would take three days, maybe—she'd hike out the door and be gone in a twinkling. Or over the wall, as agile as a monkey. It was like the call of the wild for Fiona. You've seen caged animals who pace up and down, biding their time for a chance for escape. That was Fiona. Let me outta here. We were on watch to stop girls 'absconding'—we and the other youth workers. Kept our beady eyes peeled. But Fiona was a genius. Standing before you one second, nowhere to be found the next. I once picked her up on the street, nabbed her before she could split, put her in the car and headed back to Canning Street. In Drummond Street, she suddenly shouted: "Les, slow down for a bit. Slow down." I thought she was car sick or something, so yeah, I slowed down. Fiona threw open the door, jumped out of the moving car, and zip!—she was gone. I wrenched the car into the curb, jumped out and gave chase down Drummond, into Faraday, up over Lygon. It was like one of those pursuit races they stage at velodromes in which one cyclist attempts to gain on another, and either succeeds in gaining or falls behind. I fell behind, then further behind. I could see by the expressions on the faces of people we passed real concern that the fella in hot pursuit was risking a heart seizure. And I was. A little overweight, no longer as fit as I'd once been, I had to bid Fiona adieu, the little rat.

Sometimes, though, the girls used the hostel as a sanctuary, a safe house. I had a couple of fourteen year olds nick off one morning only to return voluntarily four days later, practically battering down the front door to get in. They'd been making merfy on the streets of Carlton and Brunswick, yahoo, look at us, not a care in the world, when they met up with a couple of older kids on the run from Malmsbury Youth Training Centre. The girls and the blokes got on well for a bit, before the blokes put the hard word on my girls: get your gear off, do this and do that. The girls lost their appetite for the company of the blokes—both of them facing damn serious criminal charges—found an opening and took off back to the hostel. We had one phone call after another from the blokes, threatening murder and mayhem if the girls didn't return. The mentality of these blokes. Did they really think the girls would come rushing back into their arms after what they'd menaced them with? There's always an opportunity to turn episodes like this into the theme of a sermon to the girls. "See what happens when you give way to these impulses; bad guys galore are just itching to get their hands on rascals like you." I always resist. The girls are alienated when you harp on about their foolishness. Best let them realise the error of their ways unassisted.

Did any of them need instruction from me about the acceptable and unacceptable ways to conduct themselves in the back of a moving vehicle while changing their clothes? Let's look at it closely. I had taken four girls from the hostel up to the snow for a bit of recreation, and had told them to bring two sets of clothes, taking it for granted that they'd get the first set sopping wet in the white stuff and would need to change. Which is exactly what happened. Driving back to the city after happy times on the mountain—Buller, it was—I told the girls to put their dry set of clothes on. "Yeah, you turn the mirror to one side, well," one of then told me. "Don't want you perving." I turned the mirror and the girls got down to it. Without proper rear vision, I had to slow down, and the cars behind me were beeping their horns and flashing their lights, easy enough to ignore. But what about the waving and hilarity of the drivers as their cars overtook me? "Take a squiz and see if anything's going on in the back there," I said to my colleague from the hostel, a woman. And yeah, there was something going on. The girls, so inclined to modesty fifteen minutes earlier were now flashing brown eyes at the motorists behind. What was I going to say? Something about 'inappropriate behaviour'? Nah. I said "Cut it out!" and left it at that.

With one thing and another—girls absconding, girls attempting homicide—I came to realise that the strife these kids were dealing with wasn't likely to go away. Those two fourteen year olds, they run off and who do they hook up with? Not a couple of nice boys in the second year of uni, studying engineering. No, they find two brainless psychopaths who have only one use for them. These kids, they meet the people who endorse the reckless way they live. The abuse that fucked them up has the secondary result of making them incapable of meeting a boy who is likely to respect them, support them. The abuse has consigned them to the rubbish heap, and the only people they can talk to are other kids picking through the rubbish. And you know the most tragic thing of all? Those two boys who hooked up with my two girls, they also come from abusive homes; they've also been fucked over by life. I want to stop the cycle. I want to say to my two girls: "Respect yourself. Look for boys who have more in mind for you than exploitation." But it's all they know, abuse. They go looking for more of it.

Amongst the various frustrations I had to deal with at the hostel was the hunger of the tabloids—tabloid print and tabloid television—for stories of mayhem. Anyone who has to deal with the media knows that journos are desperate for tales that scare the daylights out of the customers. People like to be spooked. People like to think: "Oh God, it's the apocalypse". So, a news editor gets word of a girl running away from a hostel like ours and they assign a journo who knows how to paint the episode in the most lurid colours. They call me and ask what the girl was in detention for, and I say: "Came from an abusive household, needed time away from her family". The journo writes it up like this: "A fourteen-year-old girl disowned by her parents has escaped into the streets of inner Melbourne on a quest for revenge". The journo asks me if she's armed. I say: "Don't know. Don't think so." The journo writes: "Fears are held that the girl has acquired a samurai sword and an AK47 since her escape". Let me give you an example of what I'm talking about. We once organised a trip to Barwon Heads for four of the girls from the hostel; a chance for a frolic in the waves, little bit of sunbathing, a wholesome respite from the racket of the city. Nice accommodation; an entire week for the girls to enjoy themselves.

And for the first few days everything was sweet; strolls along the beach throwing chips to the seagulls; diving into the waves; building sandcastles, what have you. But on the fourth night, one of the girls slipped away in the middle of the night with mischief on her mind. She broke into a primary school, decorated the blackboards with naughty words and pictures; located a telephone in the reception area, called up the local cops and said a lot of rude things to the desk constable. The cops traced the calls to the school, sent a car round and without any grief from the girl, drove her back to the address she gave them; our address. It's part of the routine of journos to call up the local cops in the morning and ask if anything dire had happened overnight. "Let's see," says the cop on duty at the desk. "Yeah, a kid escaped from a group visiting Barwon Heads, a juvenile offender, broke into a school and made a pest of herself, we picked her up and took her back to her group." The journo rubs his hands together in glee. "Escape from Winlaton," he writes. "A midnight rampage by a dangerous female offender. God save us! The girl was off her head on proscribed substances. Lives placed in jeopardy. Barwon Heads at the mercy of a maniac." And so on. And the girl, Michelle, hadn't escaped from Winlaton, the detention centre for juvenile girls, for God's sake. Having thrown a panic into the populace, the journo leans back in his chair with a satisfied smile on his face, leaving me to deal with the fallout. Bloody hell.

Over those years at the hostel (I should have mentioned that it was run by the Melbourne City Mission), I was on a vertical learning curve. Every single day provided me with experiences that educated me, mostly lessons in juvenile psychology, but also in the knowledge of the system that governed these kids, and knowledge of the law; what lawyers you could count on, what beaks would give a kid the benefit of the doubt (most); and the likely places where the absconding kids would hole up. It's a whole subculture, and I became a scholar of it. But you know what I remember more than anything from those years at Carlton? I remember the distress and trouble in the eyes of the kids. I remember those days when the kids looked at me and the candid look on their faces was this: "Why bother about me, Les? It's good of you, but face it, I'm fucked." I never once conceded any such thing. I mentioned earlier that I had exactly the right resources to do this job with the kids. Amongst my resources—maybe the most important thing of all—was that I kept hope alive in my heart for each and every one of the little buggers. They could never be so sly and sneaky and deceitful that I felt like giving up. They could never be so abusive towards me that I became alienated. I kept at it. It's something I'm proud of, as you can see. I kept at it.

And there were moments of rich comedy. I should mention that. Let me tell you about one of my clients, a little redheaded nong who'd decided on a career as a burglar—all well and good except he was hopeless at it. He was in my hands because he'd been nicked trying to steal an organ from a school out in the west. A real organ, bloody big thing, way beyond his capabilities. He triggered an alarm and the cops arrived to discover him trying to manhandle the organ out of a door it wouldn't fit through. I took him to see a barrister, Tony Isaacs, top bloke, appeared for lots of kids from out west. Tony has a look at the kid, shakes his head as if it's manifest immediately that he's dealing with a dozy nitwit. Then he has a look at the kid's record. Five previous burglaries, nicked each time. Tony shakes his head, adjusts his specs. "What made you decide on the organ?" Tony said. "Just on the face of it, a bastard of a thing to get home, and a bastard to sell. Did you give all that any thought?" The kid gives a sheepish grin and a shrug. Tony goes on: "Here's my advice. You're crap at burglaries. You might want to turn your attention elsewhere. How about holding up banks? How's that appeal?"

7

You Are My Sunshine

Back in the middle decades of the twentieth century, Sunshine Council was run like a mafia fiefdom. I don't mean to say that it was home to crooks from Calabria and Naples, but it was run according to the same ethics the mafia observed, which is to say, "What's in it for me?" And boy, was it rough. The hard men of the council drew the line exactly nowhere. They considered it their God-given right to make as much dough out of their stint on the council as they possibly could. Turf wars broke out. Johnny A was trying to skim something off Johnny B's racket. Legs were broken, noses broken, skulls broken. All of this came to an end, temporarily, when the Hamer government dismissed the council in the '70s. Hamer said: "Bad guys. The only reason they're in local government is to line their pockets." The bad guys protested with all the force of their lungs: "Who's a bad guy? Me? You must be joking. I'm a Christian saint. Everything for the poor. Never skimmed a zack in my life!"

When I came over to the Sunshine Council as a youth worker in 1984, the old bad guys had been replaced by new bad guys. Same rackets, same muscle. I caught a whiff of what was going on and kept well away. I was a babe in the woods when it came to this sort of corruption and how-do-you-do, and I was left alone. People on the make immediately recognise others ready to join up. They looked at me and thought: "A goody-goody". And really, where was the money in youth work? It wasn't as if the budget for what I was doing in my area of the shire—Braybrook—was full of cream ready to be scooped off by the hard men. The budget was rubbish.

Now, part of my brief was to counsel individuals and families enduring hardship: make them aware of services, help those who needed a bit more knowledge of the law, such as: "Yeah, that's right, theft is illegal; they'll throw you in the clink". But as a matter of fact, most of the Braybrook folk who came to me were after something more practical, such as food. Or food and money for the rent. Or food and money for the rent and shoes for the kids. I'd grown up in Braybrook, which was the reason they gave it to me, my old hometown, but I'd never experienced and had rarely even seen the sort of poverty that I was now witnessing. I mean, this was Third World stuff, lives lived at the level you'd find in refugee camps. I spoke to mothers who were forced to feed their kids dog food, and who knew the tastiest choices amongst the cheaper brands. Also, whole families that hit the streets on the night before rubbish collection so that they could go through the rubbish bins and fossick about for anything edible. A couple of kids who came my way—little blokes, they were—were enjoying the benefits of one government program or another that allowed them to eat cooked food in their household. Until the government threw a few quid the way of this family, those kids had never seen a gas flame on the stove. They were feeling triumphant on the day I saw them because their mum had been able to fry potato skins for them for brekkie before they headed off to school. It was a scavenger subculture, with its skills and dodges and specialist knowledge. Even its own ethics, such as keeping to a certain territory on rubbish collection night, never infringing on an area that belonged to your comrades. In my home when I was a kid, I never missed a meal, never knew hunger. And we were never shoeless, my brothers and my sister and I. Were never served dog food.

So, facing this scavenger class, I was well and truly shocked. I thought: "How the hell do these people keep going?" Well, they did keep going, as the poor always keep going, everywhere in the world. They set their sights much lower than those who have a bit of dosh jingling in their pockets. They don't ask much of life. But now I want to tell you a tale that provides an insight into the souls of these do-without people; a sort of corrective. I had amongst my clients in Braybrook a family that was in never-ending strife. Woeful. A week never passed without me going around to the family's house in the most ramshackle part of this ramshackle town to sort out one crisis or another.

One fine day, a kid in the family—a boy of about fourteen—came home from school howling his eyes out. The kids in his class had been teasing him about his tattered clothes, then went further and gave him a hiding. You'd think in Braybrook, where everyone's short of a quid, that there'd be a sort of base level of sympathy each for the other. But maybe not so much amongst kids. Because kids can distinguish between levels of poverty to a very fine degree. The kids who have shoes without holes in them enjoy a feeling of superiority over those kids who have shoes with worn-through soles. And the kids who can bring a sandwich to school for lunch give those who have nothing a hard time. This kid I'm talking about, he had shoes held together with string, and nothing at all in his lunchbox. So, there he is crying his eyes out, and when his mum and dad hear the story they charge down to the school intending to dish out knuckle justice to the merciless little buggers who'd made their boy cry. They get to the school, where there are still some of these bullies hanging around, as well as their parents who've come to pick them up. My little kid's parents get stuck into the parents of the bullies and within minutes there's a riot, fists flying everywhere, and the cops are called, charges laid. The parents of my little kid have to appear before the magistrate a few weeks later, and they do, together with all their kids including one little tacker who doesn't belong to them, a homeless kid they've taken in through the goodness of their hearts. I'm at court to speak up on behalf of the family, and when the magistrate asks me to introduce the various family members, I tell him the names, kids' names, too, but when I reach the homeless kid I have to say that this little bloke doesn't actually belong to the mum and dad.

"Then whose child is he, Mr Twentyman? Just an anonymous waif?"

"No, Your Honour. He's been adopted by the family. He's homeless."

Your Honour looks flabbergasted.

"Are you saying, Mr Twentyman, that these people, impecunious as they are, have added to their burden by taking in a stray?"

"That's about the size of it, Your Honour."

"So, the poor are looking after the poor?"

"That's right, Your Honour."

"Extraordinary."

When I started at Sunshine Council, I was the only youth worker employed there. For a thousand years before I arrived, nobody bothered. So, there were none of the guidelines that are in force these days. For example, working in pairs. Now, it has been said regarding my tubby figure that two reasonably trim human beings could be fashioned from me, a very rude thing to say and I scorn those who made the comment. But you can't fashion a pair of youth workers out of the sole youth worker in Sunshine, no matter how hard you try. So, my sorties into the impoverished households of Braybrook were all solo. Braybrook, great place, some of the most generous people you could ever meet—but also some of the most violent. Domestic violence was particularly rife, mostly the old man biffing the wife, or biffing the kids, or biffing both. I'd say to the person on reception at the council offices: "If I'm not back in two hours, send out a search party". No mobile phones back then, and most of the Braybrook households had no landline phone—people couldn't afford them. So, if I encountered strife, threats to life and limb, I had to find a public telephone box to call for back-up (not that there was any back-up) and all the telephone boxes were buggered. (A curious thing, but in rough areas, even when there is no prospect of getting money from a device, the telephone boxes are always vandalised, as if the poor old box was guilty of some offence just by standing lonely and forlorn on a street corner.) Now, if you put yourself between a husband and the wife he's thumping, or between the kids and the dad (sometimes the mum) you're asking for trouble. But that was very often the only alternative I had, if I wanted to forestall murder. Angry people, they don't think straight. I might say: "Mate, if you hit her again, you'll be up on a homicide charge". They don't care. Same thing applies in other jobs. Nurses, doctors, cops—they all encounter violence, homicidal hysteria. I've been whacked, had knives aimed at my breadbasket, kicked in the goolies. What I had to think at times like that was: "Les, old pal, you'll survive this, you'll get home tonight and pour yourself a scotch. It'll all fade away."

You have to believe you've got a guardian angel who'll save you from any real harm. I'll give you an example. When I was working in the girls' hostel in Canning Street, Carlton—well before Sunshine—I had a girl in my care by the name of Tessa, fifteen years old, on the game. She ran off from the hostel and I didn't see her again until one evening down in St. Kilda. I'd stopped for a burger in Fitzroy Street and by chance, Tessa walked in. "Les, how you going. Good to see ya." We continued the conversation out on the footpath. Then her pimp turned up, full of aggro and spleen as pimps always are, and he said some unkind and unpleasant things to me, taking me for a customer who was being difficult—something like that. In a courteous and professional manner, I told him to fuck off. He pulled a knife, slashed me on my arm. Tessa jumped in between us, pushed the pimp away: "He's my social worker, you moron!" Tessa, she was the guardian angel on duty that evening. Without her initiative, the pimp/moron would have had another go at me. For me, it's an article of faith that something or someone will save me from the worst that can happen.

Oh, and death threats. Always death threats. It's one of the themes of the caper. Most death threats, you can shrug off. People get upset with you and before they can think a bit more about it, they're telling you that they'll cut your throat.

You usually mutter: "Yeah, yeah, whatever". But some of the threats are serious. The best predictor of the seriousness of a death threat is previous form. Some bloke wants to murder you, and it turns out he's had a go at murdering people in the past—okay, show the idiot the respect he deserves. After all, murder as a way of dealing with a grievance has a long, long history, going right back to Cain in the Bible, who gave his brother Abel, a lethal whack on the noggin.

I had an unsavoury character make a death threat in my Braybrook days with the Sunshine Council. I thought, ho hum, another day, another evil bastard who wants to do away with me. I spoke to the cops who said it was dead serious this time. "This bloke'll cut your tripes out and sell them at the Vic market, so be wary, Les." The solution the cops came up with was for me to move to Brighton. Brighton? How come Brighton? "This bloke", the cop in charge told me, "it would be beneath his dignity to carve anyone up in Brighton. Too genteel. And he never goes south of the river." Okay, it's odd, but homicidal lunatics also have eccentricities, so I accepted the logic of the proposition and moved into rental accommodation in Brighton. And was left untroubled. But people who knew me—people I *thought* knew me—were dismayed. "What are you doing, Les? *Brighton*? You can't live in Brighton. It's full of toffs, Les! People will think you've sold out." I had no idea how deep people's prejudices went. Brighton to me was just a place that gave me some protection from bad guys. It turns out that there are whole catalogues of things that people can base aversions on. You live in Brighton, you must be an enemy of the working class. You drive a Merc, you must be a factory owner employing child labour down the mines. You wear a Henry Bucks shirt—obviously, a Lib. You know, all of these supposed markers of privilege give me the shits. I've said before in these pages that I've known truly fine human beings who own mansions, and I've known total arseholes who operate out of a fibro shack in Airport West. The time came—and this I find unbelievable—when I was running for state parliament as an Independent. The Labor Party backroom boys pulled up this file that proved I'd once lived in Brighton. "Will you look at this? Les Twentyman, says he's the battler's friend, used to live in bloody Brighton, two-storey mansion, heated Olympic-size swimming pool, underpaid servants handing out glasses of Chateau Rothschild." Do me a favour.

So, there I am in Braybrook, doing the best I can as a solo operator, trying to understand more as I went along. Because there were very, very few youth workers in the whole of Australia at that time—the early 1980s. I said, "trying to understand more as I went along" in order to avoid saying, "making it up as I went along", which sounds a little suss. But in all honesty, I *was* making it up as I went along, attempting to match the skills I had with the tasks that came my way. Not simply my skills, but my natural sympathies. I've often been promoted as a great buddy of the battler, and that's true, but it's a really a clichéd way of saying that I grasp the problems my clients face every day.

Look, it's a big, busy society, the broad Australian community, and you're expected to figure out the many paths you can take and fashion a life for yourself that allows you to follow this path or that. It's not superhumanly difficult, but there are a number of people who just can't figure it out. The great big busy community is a puzzle to them; it frustrates them so badly that the dreams they have always seem beyond reach. Even the small dreams, the modest dreams. Some kid of eighteen wants a car. Okay, he'll need to sit for a learner's permit first, pay his dough across the counter, learn the road rules, then find someone with a full licence who can teach him about driving.

Six months later, he goes for his licence, pays his dough across the counter, takes his test, and fails because he went three kilometres above the limit coming down a hill. Now the mindset this kid's got after a disadvantaged upbringing makes him feel that the officer telling him he's failed his test is picking on him, doesn't like the look of his face, whatever; gross injustice. He's always close to anger, and this pisses him off. But he swallows his anger and makes a new appointment to go for his licence, six months off. In the meantime, he listens to his mates who tell him: "Man, just grab a car, change the plates, don't take any more shit". This sense of the injustice of life he harbours, together with peer pressure, together with the fact that he can't find the dough for a second test, all adds up to grand theft auto. He gets caught—well, of course—goes up before the magistrate, gets put on diversion because this is a first offence, can't go for his licence for a further twelve months. And okay, it's the kid's fault, but the culture of privation he's grown up with leaves him with less patience, less goodwill towards the community, fewer options for success than a kid going for his licence in Glen Waverley. Now, I get it. I can see what's got into the kid's head. And when he inevitably comes my way, I never attempt to lecture him about his obligations to society, or any nonsense like that. I say: "Temptation got the better of you, mate. Well, let's see what we can do."

I'm out there each day in Braybrook, armed with my sympathies. But I wouldn't have you go away from this session of reading with the idea that Les was incapable of finding fault with his clientele. Bloody hell no. It was the parents of some of my clients who shocked me most, sometimes sickened me. Let me tell you about Doris, who was deeply religious and totally evil. She was the mother of Des, wife of Fred, both of them victims of Vampire Doris. When I got to know the son, Des, he was in his early teens. Doris had contacted the Sunshine Council welfare people, demanding that her son be locked up in a juvenile detention centre. She would have preferred Alcatraz, but this was Australia and we didn't have any fortified island prisons for kids. And what was it that had driven Doris to this hysterical conclusion about her boy? She had found what she believed to be semen stains on his bedsheets. He was bound for hell. Attempts were made to explain to Doris that it was pretty much a normal thing for semen stains to appear on the bedsheets of fourteen-year-old boys. But that was just Doris's point—it shouldn't be thought of as 'normal'; it should be considered depraved.

I was put in contact with Doris and I tried to make her understand that what Des would endure during a term in a youth detention centre would make semen stains on his sheets seem practically wholesome. No, no, no—the boy had to be dealt with harshly if that was needed to save him from damnation. Her husband, Fred, couldn't be relied on to administer punishment because he was (as Doris insisted) 'weak'. So far as I could tell, Fred was not so much 'weak' as profoundly demoralised, and looked like he wished he could die and be buried and never see Doris again. "No, Doris, we're not going to lock your son up," I told her. "Go home, calm down, bake some biscuits and give half a dozen to your boy, and a kiss," I told her.

Now, the ordeal of being raised by Doris maybe took its toll on Des, because a little while later he involved himself in some petty criminal stuff, perhaps hoping that he *would* be locked up, away from his mum. I spoke to Des, told him he'd have to front the beak, but that I would be in court to advocate for him. The magistrate, Francine McNiff, was a woman of great intelligence and compassion. She listened to the police account, listened to my testimony, and released Des to me on a one-dollar bond. Doris was in court for the hearing, hoping with all her heart that her boy would be sentenced to five hundred lashes with a cat o' nine tails and ten years' hard labour. She jumped to her feet when Francine gave her ruling, complaining that Les Twentyman was not at all the sort of person who should be given responsibility for a boy's welfare, or anyone's. "He drinks!" she cried out. "He's been seen in the pub, drinking *beer*!" She voiced the word, 'beer' as if it were a concoction brewed by the witches from Macbeth. Francine said calmly: "Madam, you would be most unlikely to find anyone in this courtroom who doesn't drink beer, or perhaps scotch".

Des stayed with his adult sister after his court appearance, either because his mother wouldn't take him back, or simply because he wanted to, needed to. A condition attached to the magistrate's ruling was that Des had to be home at his sister's place by 10 o'clock each night, for a certain period. Maybe his sister didn't take the curfew seriously because when Des's maniacal mum stopped by one night to see her daughter and son, Des wasn't home. It was 10.05, and the mum went into a frothing fit, telephoned the cops to report that her son had breached his bail conditions. The cops wouldn't lock him up, the mum's pleading notwithstanding. I eventually lost track of Des and his demon mum, but dear God, I hope with all my heart that things improved. I include this tale simply as an example of life amongst the muddled and the put-upon, but also as an example of what some of the kids I knew had to endure. Okay, it's true, you could be a kid living in a comfy suburb and still be cursed with a half-mad mother, or father, for that matter. But the thing is, poor Des couldn't think to himself: "I'll put up with this for a couple more years, graduate from Xavier, get into uni, move into a share house, and after a few years of study, I'll be an engineer". The world is a bigger place for kids in the comfy suburbs. Disaster isn't always just that one step behind you. For kids like Des, with parents (or in Des's case, one of the parents) who have no goodwill towards you, let alone love to share with you, imagination itself becomes stunted, and they're unable to think their way out of a bad life into a better one.

Other parents I came across went about their parenting in a half-arsed, incompetent way, without actually having the vile influence of Des's vile mum. Let me tell you the story (and I'm telling it for a purpose, as you'll see if you'll just be patient for a few minutes!) of a mum by the name of—well, by the name of what? I can't use her real name. Okay, by the name of Mary. Mary lived not in Braybrook but in Sunshine, but I was called in, all the same. Mary's fourteen-year-old son Henry (as we'll call him) was, as they say, 'known to the police'. Well, that's putting it mildly. He was 'known to the police' in the way that Ned Kelly was 'known to the police' in his day. And not only Henry, but his mum and dad and brother. Henry was not vicious; none of the family was bad in that way. But crime was their thing. It was a career choice. I suppose in the past, Henry's mum and dad and brother had reflected on the path ahead in life, and each had thought: "You know what? I'm good at larceny, I know how to frighten the bejesus out of people, I'm obviously suited to a life of crime". Anyway, Henry had lost his cool at school one fine day and gone berserk and smashed anything in his path. So, he was sent home. "Henry, you're a bad, bad boy. Now go home and don't come back until we invite you back, which might be in a hundred years."

I'm called in, as I say, so I dawdle over to Henry's place, his mum answers the door, quite charming, dressed in tights with a leopard skin print, bulging cleavage, puffing away on her five hundredth fag of the day. "And your name is? Les Twentyman? Okay Les, delighted to meet you, and what can I do for you? Call me Mary." Henry's there on the sofa, pays me not the slightest attention, eyes on the telly. He has an asthma pump that he brings to his nostrils every minute or so. I say: "Well, Mary, it appears young Henry here has been on a rampage at school, smashed up this, smashed up that, bad business." Mary says: "Oh yeah, Henry told me about that. That's no good, is it?" I'm about to tell Mary all the ways in which 'that's no good' when her elder son, Barry, arrives home with a couple of mates. Barry's not best pleased to see me there chatting to his mum. He frowns, cocks his chin, gives the impression that he might knock my block off if I persist with the visit. I say: "Well, I'd better get moving along, long day, need to get home, chop the firewood".

The next day I heard that the cops were on the trail of Barry and his mate. And no wonder. The story that emerged over the weeks that followed my visit to Mary was this: Barry and his buddies are out on the streets, minding their own business, when a woman runs from a house screaming her head off, closely pursued by a roughnut threatening to reduce her to hamburger when he catches her. Barry, being a gentleman, and his mates, also gentlemen, make a decision to intervene on the side of the woman. Which they do. But the intervention—well, they used a bit too much force, whacking Roughnut over the head with a length of fence paling which came to hand. Barry looks down at Roughnut. Something's not right, which is to say, Roughnut's not breathing. And doesn't have a pulse. Meaning, he's dead. The Good Samaritans cover the body with torn-up grass and hurry home to tell mum of the incident. That's what they had on their minds when they walked in and found me in my tête-à-tête with Mary. After I left (so the story continues), Barry gave the details of the homicide to mum, who says: "Fucking hell! Are you sure he's dead?"

"Yeah, Mum, we're sure."

"Check his pulse?"

"Yeah, Mum, checked his pulse."

"Covered him up?"

"Yeah, Mum, covered him up."

"Okay, show me."

Mum is conveyed to the corpse of Roughnut. Verifies that he's not breathing and that he can no longer be said to have a pulse. Mum says: "Get a car, put him in it, take him somewhere and dump him".

Sound advice. The boys drive the car west, towards Ballarat, with Roughnut in the boot. Dump him in the Lerderderg State Park. If you get yourself murdered out in Sunshine, Braybrook, you're likely to be disposed of in the

Lerderderg. It's the first dense bush you reach as you head away west from the city. And such was the fate of Roughnut.

But one way or another, the cops catch up with Mary's boy and his mates, and they're carted off to court. A barrister is appointed to represent them. In the entrance hall before her boys front the judge, Mary wanders over to the barrister with a question. "It's just murder, isn't it?" she says. And the barrister tells her yes, the charge is murder. "Good-o," says Mary, who'd been worried that car theft and maybe a few other charges were in the brief. "Murder we can cope with." Well, the barrister was going to claim in court that his clients were trying to do good, save a woman from being beaten, pure accident that the fence paling came into contact with Roughnut's brainbox, and really, Your Honour, these boys should have a medal struck for them. These mitigating factors did the trick. Homicide—no. Manslaughter, yes. Five years, two with good behaviour.

Now, the point I want to make is that there's more than one way to go about your parenting. Mary did her best. She didn't raise the boys to revere the rule of law in a civil society, sure, but she cared for the kids. I can understand that. I don't need every parent in Australia to subscribe to the one set of rules. But I do need them to care, make the effort, get up off the sofa and check out the body, find a barrister, make sure the kids get to court, visit them in Pentridge, bake some scones to take. I need that. That I can work with.

I recall another parent with an unorthodox approach to parenting, and I'll just reinforce the point I was making by telling you what happened when my car was broken into one night back in Sunshine Council days. At that time, I kept only very basic written records of interviews with kids and their parents. It made clients very jittery to have someone writing down what they said. These kids, the only people they'd ever seen writing anything in their lives, outside school, were cops, taking down statements. So it was my practice to just listen, then scribble something into a notebook later. But then it was pointed out to me that I needed to have something to show if I was called on later to explain myself. Or if I disappeared into the Lerderderg State Park, something to show what I'd been working on, who I'd been speaking to. So I got myself a Dictaphone and I'd warble a few things into the mic every so often. I'd leave the Dictaphone in the car overnight, and so it happened that when my car was done over, the thieves took the device. I came out in the morning, saw the damage, and the first thing I thought about was the Dictaphone—the Dictaphone that wasn't in the car any longer. It happened to be an awkward time to have the thing stolen, because I'd been speaking to a couple of clients about their drug deals, and the stuff they'd confided to me and that I'd confided to the Dictaphone, was dynamite. I went about in a running sweat for days, anticipating a visit from a couple of big strong blokes who'd invite me to a short tour of the Lerderderg. If you're in the wholesale narcotics business, your default negotiating strategy is homicide. These guys, they'd kill you even if there's little need; it's just part of the craft.

Not long after the theft, I was at a venue of hospitality in South Melbourne, a pub in simple parlance, enjoying a glass of the chilled article. A bloke I'd never seen before sauntered up to me and said: "Are you Les Twentyman?" This is a bloke in his forties, a little rough around the edges. There was no hint of a threat in his question, and since I was beginning to enjoy the influence of the beer, I simply said: "Yes, I am, as a matter of fact". It wasn't uncommon for strangers to wander up to me and introduce themselves; people who'd seen me on the news or some current affairs show. I was getting a fair bit of exposure on the telly mostly because of my willingness to speak about the plight of troubled kids in the west, and when I was on telly I made it my business to call a spade a spade and a chicken a chook. This bloke in the pub, he went on to ask me if I'd had my car broken into recently. In a slightly warier manner, I said: "Well, yes—yes I have".

This would-be new friend nodded his head. "Yeah, that was my son. Sorry it happened to be your car."

"Well, what can you say? It's done, now."

"Yeah, it's done. Now, would you like to buy your Dictaphone back?"

"Buy my Dictaphone back?"

"Yeah. Whaddya think?"

What I thought was that I'd be well advised to not make a big thing out of this. If I seemed avid, this bloke might well suggest an auction, get a few of his mates to gather round and raise higher and higher bids. So I produced my most charming smile and said that there was nothing much on the Dictaphone, and I was happy to let the thing go. We parted none the worse for the experience.

Once again, this is parenting that I can accept. The dad sees an opening to enhance his boy's revenue, approaches me with this offer of a lifetime, the offer is reluctantly declined, the dad will later have to tell his boy Les Twentyman didn't come through with any dough. Now, if the dad had said to me; "It was my boy who took your Dictaphone, I'm full of remorse for his behaviour, here's your device and I hope you can forgive the scallywag," I would have thought, "Well and good," but I would also have been astonished. It happens that knocking stuff off is, often enough, a family business in Sunshine and Braybrook. And if it's a family business, then the boy who took the Dictaphone is probably not being abused by his dad. That's okay. I could tell by the dad's appearance that he wasn't hanging out, desperate for a whack of smack; it was just business as usual. You can see I'm making a confession here. I'm not about to take the moral high ground when it comes to crime. It's only abuse that gets into my guts, because that's where real harm is done. You remember what Jesus said about the poor—that they are always with us? Well, I say that crime is always with us. I'm not on a mission to wipe out larceny.

Now, one way and another I was getting a fair bit of publicity as a youth worker at Sunshine. My name was in newspaper articles, I was on the radio, on the telly. And I had a few critics who thought that I was an egomaniac. But here's the thing: I saw from very early on that what the kids I was dealing with were facing, was being made invisible. You could live in Melbourne all your life and attain an advanced age without ever having seen a homeless kid, a kid in a lane with a needle in his arm, or a kid wandering in a daze along the footpath mumbling incoherently. None of that. In most of the suburbs of Melbourne, kids don't shoot up in lanes, and they don't go off mumbling to themselves. It's just in maybe ten suburbs that this sort of heartbreaking stuff goes down. Let me ask a question, a spontaneous question of the readers of this book, My Life and Hard Times, the Les Twentyman Saga, or whatever it ends up being titled. Have you, Reader, ever been to Braybrook? Have you ever driven through Braybrook? Have you ever been to Sunshine? Maybe some of my readers have driven through Braybrook and Sunshine, but how many have parked their car, got out and walked around in those suburbs? I'm going to suggest that very, very few have ever put their foot to the ground in Braybrook. So, it's like this. If those kids are invisible to most of the inhabitants of Melbourne, what hope have they got to attract money for programs that help them out of the gutter? I made it my job to tear away this veil of invisibility. I wanted to say: "Okay, you see these hell-holes on the news in Third World countries, frightening places, poverty, starvation. What about my patch? What about Braybrook? What about Sunshine?

Because I can tell you that there are hell-holes in these suburbs that would make you weep."

The kids can't publicise their situation. Staying alive is a big enough task for them. I saw early on that the kids needed a spokesperson, and I thought: "Les, that would be you". And I discovered that I was good at it. Well, when I say 'good at it' what I mean is that I have a gift for not shutting up once I start. I don't get tongue-tied, I get up a head of steam and I keep chuffing ahead. People in the media introduce me as a bloke who 'tells it like it is', and yeah, I do, but saying that I speak my mind is putting it too simplistically. What I do is make the points the situation calls for. People who always 'speak their minds' can be pains in the arse, full of self-regard. Whatever you think of me, don't think of me as self-important, but just as I said—a bloke who makes the points the situation calls for. And not for myself, but on behalf of kids who don't have any eloquence.

The publicity that comes my way, yeah, it does tend to suggest that the only youth worker in Australia that the media wants to talk to is me. And this must give the public the idea that I'm a genius at what I do. Well, I'm not. I'm just a bloke who works hard at what he does. And the same is true for most youth workers. Well, of course it is. Nobody gets into this game to make themselves enough money to instal a swimming pool and a bar. People who become youth workers are highly motivated, and most have big hearts. I'm thinking of my one-time colleague,

Jim Markovski, as a special example. I came to know Jim when the number of youth workers at Sunshine Council had been increased. You couldn't have met a bloke more concerned about the kids in his care. If Jim was on your side, you had the best corner man in the game. We went up to Queensland one time with eighteen kids in our care, me and Jim, and I have to tell you that caring for all those kids—and some real scallywags amongst them, you bet—called for true commitment. We were in tents up on the coast somewhere, me in a tent solo because of my snoring (which at least had the benefit of keeping the goannas away, something the kids realised after a few nights of enforced hosting of these scaly creatures in their sleeping bags, they wanted to be nice and close to the Twentyman canvas after that) and Jim keeping an ear out the whole night for strife. Now, in situations like this, caring for eighteen kids, some of those in charge might say: "Okay, amuse yourselves, don't bother me," and settle down with a six-pack and the radio turned to the Doomben races. Not Jim. He stayed alert and engaged the whole time. And Jim, his level of commitment was pretty typical of the youth workers I've known.

I've already mentioned the one thing I have that most youth workers don't have, the only thing, and that's the ability to talk forever. If I was an astronaut and they strapped me into a space capsule and sent me to the moon, I wouldn't be saying, "One small step for a man, one giant step for mankind." No, no, I'd emerge from the capsule in my spacesuit saying: "Listen, where's the bloody Minister for Youth Affairs, I need to talk to him about a couple of kids down in Braybrook getting the rough end of the pineapple; I have to sort some things out". That's it. Just the mouth. Any other youth worker with a mouth like mine would attract the same level of media attention.

You know, a television crew from Channel Seven came down to the Sunshine Shire Offices to interview me some years ago. Wanted a few words of the Twentyman wisdom. The cameraman, who'd been part of the crew for a dozen earlier interviews, asked one of my colleagues, the late Jo Mannion, if she ever felt jealous about Les being the go-to bloke whenever the media wanted a bit of a rant to put to air. Jo said: "No way. Every time you people talk to Les, he faces the sack for sounding off. Me, I've got a mortgage. I wouldn't risk it. So go to Les, by all means." Oh, and I must mention what John James told me—CEO of Sunshine Council at about the same time that Jo made her very pertinent remarks to the cameraman. He said that there were two councillors at every shire meeting who could never agree on anything—Jean Boles and Jan White. If Jean said: "Nice day," to the assembled councillors, Jan would say: "Nice day, my arse. It's a rotten day". If Jean asked for tea, Jan would ask for coffee. They rubbed each other up the wrong way—temperamental opposites. But there was one thing they did agree on, one thing and one thing only, and it was this: Les Twentyman must be sacked. When John told me, I felt honoured to be singled out in this way.

So in a sense, I recognised that I had to become an entrepreneur of an unusual sort. We think of entrepreneurs as high-flyers dealing in millions with a mansion overlooking the Yarra above Alexandra Avenue, never out of their Giorgio Armani clobber, a client stable of the rich and famous. I was an entrepreneur for the muddled and homeless, never out of my Kmart jeans, with a client list of the abused, the drug-addled and half-mad. And I wasn't trying to get my clients five million up front and twenty percent of the gate; instead, a hundred bucks to help with the rent and another thirty to cover breakfast for a week. But in a way, the skills you'd need to stage a tour for the Rolling Stones were the same skills needed to get a four-unit accommodation block built for the homeless. Persuasion, problem solving, making sure your client shows up at such-and-such a time in such-and-such a place. I can't be apologetic about courting the media, considering that it's always been nothing more than a means to an end.

This entrepreneurial dimension to the job became even less acceptable to the people who employed me once the Great Big Spooky Council Amalgamation Event of 1994 unfolded. This was Jeff Kennett's idea, the amalgamations. He wanted to make local government less of a mess than it was—and yeah, it *was* a mess: too many councils, too much duplication, too many small-scale empires being lorded over by small-scale emperors. But it happened that Jeff's amalgamations coincided with the Professionalisation of Everything. A bloke like me without a degree in

Youth Services Administration would never have been employed under the new rules. Councils, every one of them, had an academically trained CEO, academically trained everyone—you could barely get a job as a tea lady at a town hall without a diploma in Tea Trolley Administration and Biscuit Best Practice. Now, all this training, all of these degrees, it might have worked out well except that the training didn't include empathy or compassion. People couldn't do a damned thing without a Mission Statement and a list of expected 'outcomes' that could be cross-referenced with 'desired results'. It was a power thing. A new class of local government graduates had evolved and, to protect their status, they wanted an agreed set of credentials to negotiate hiring. A territorial thing. The people we saw come to the newly-created Brimbank Council (made up of the old Sunshine Council and a few others), yeah, some of them good at their jobs, but most not. If you'd embraced a career in local government, you wanted a job in one of the spruce new shires like City of Port Phillip, that took in yuppie enclaves such as St. Kilda and Middle Park; or City of Yarra, taking in Melbourne; City of Stonnington, with Malvern at its heart; City of Bayside, centred on Brighton and Sandringham; City of Boroondara, with genteel Camberwell in the middle. If you ended up in Brimbank, you thought of it as a stop along the way to grander things.

Yeah, talking, chatting, nattering, sounding off—all of great benefit to me over the years. Of course, it's a difficult accomplishment to summarise on a CV. Special Skills: Can talk under five metres of concrete. Of course, it also depends on what you talk about. Back in my Sunshine days, I exploited my knowledge of sports to engage the listener. What do you think kids of the sort I had in my care were interested in? Plato? Aristotle? Quantum mechanics? No, they were interested in sport, food, sex and drugs. Didn't have much to say about food and sex, and anything I had to say about drugs would have to be brief (i.e. use clean sharps; check the dose; shoot up with a friend, if you're going to shoot up at all) but sport, a terrific subject, even with the girls. I'd tell them about experiences I had while coaching; terrific sportspeople I'd met; anecdotes, some of them scurrilous. It's like this. I'm sitting opposite a kid who barely gets an hour's worth of love and attention from his parents in a month; a kid who's tried a whole smorgasbord of gear, and is left with very limited ambitions for his life, her life. The kid's profoundly sceptical; you can't rely on bullshit, on sermons. But if anything good's going to come out of the meeting, there has to be engagement; genuine human connection. So, I start nattering about AFL teams, the ladder, and so on. I manage to get out of the kid that he or she supports the Scraggers, the Bullies. I say: "Yeah? So, you'll know Dougie Hawkins, I bet? He's a mate of mine, Dougie. I can tell you a funny story about Dougie and Mick McGuane". I tell the funny story, and we connect, the kid and me. And the story? It was about the circus. Was it Ashton's? Anyway, the circus came to town back in 1990, the year Collingwood won the flag, coached by Lethal Leigh. Dougie and I and Mick McGuane from the Pies, were invited to appear on a morning breakfast show to promote Dougie's book about life in footy, and also Dougie's role in sponsoring kids in strife. The show was being broadcast from the big top for the sake of spectacle. The producer wanted Dougie and Mick to go into the lions' cage with the beasts. I thought: "Oh yeah?" Dougie, not all that keen, asked if the lions had been sedated. The producer asked the lion tamer. The lion tamer pulled up the cuff of his daks and showed us a prosthetic lower limb. "Sedated, my arse," he said. "One of those buggers chewed off me leg!" I thought: "This is bullshit!" Dougie said: "You know what? Forget it." But the producer said he had to get Dougie and Mick into the lions' cage if he was going to run the promo. Dougie and Mick looked at each other, grimaced, and stepped into the cage. I have to tell you, I expected them both to die, slowly, from chewing, and I thought: "So this is it, Dougie, my friend, all the way from Footscray where a lion has never been seen, only to die on national television when the King of the Beasts sinks his choppers into your throat". Mick and Dougie stood trembling in that cage until the producer told them they could exit. I don't think Dougie ever moved faster in his life, not even on the wing at the Western Oval.

I had a whole catalogue of anecdotes about AFL players to draw from. And players of other sports, too—basketball, cricket, etc. There was this little bloke, Nathan, ten years old. He created havoc at school one day, went spare, and

I was called in to 'talk some sense into the boy', by which his teachers meant, shout at him for a prolonged period. Well, that was going to prove futile. I never shout at people, except politicians. I sat down with him in the staffroom and he glared back at me with eyes full of resentment. I said: "How you going, Nathan?" And Nathan gave me a variation of the resentful glare, the message of which was: "Fuck you". But I'd been told that the only thing he truly gave himself to was cricket. I said: "You know what I heard, Nathan? Tell me if I'm right. I heard that you've got a big thing for cricket. When I heard that, I thought, 'Good-o, I'll have something to talk to him about.'

"Big fan of the game myself. Got a mate in the test team, Rodney Hogg. So, what do you think, Nathan? Looking pretty good, our boys? D'ya reckon we'll keep the ashes?"

Nathan was paying more and more attention. The bitter and resentful look had faded in his eyes. He began to speak to me in sentences of four or five words, but only on the subject of cricket. And the reason for that wasn't hard to understand. He was good at cricket, the best player in the school, and he knew the rules in all their complexity, grasped their logic and purpose. At home, the rules of the game were a shocking mess. Nathan's mother went off every weekend to make merry with her new boyfriend, and she'd leave Nathan in charge of his four-year-old brother. When a mother does that, it's the same thing as saying: "I don't love you, I don't care much what happens to you". And that's a horrible burden for a ten-year-old kid to carry around. I was engaging Nathan on an arena where he was a master. Meanwhile, the teachers are waiting outside the open door waiting to hear me shouting at the kid and threatening him with the rack and thumbscrews if he didn't start behaving. I mean, bloody hell.

This waiting outside the door while I dealt with some kid guilty of a minor transgression was common enough. At the home of the kid, it was the habit of the parents to listen in on the conversation I was having with Junior, and the number of complaints that got back to the council about this Twentyman bloke talking about footy and cricket and boxing and basketball instead of invoking the wrath of God. My defence was always the same: "Do you want me to talk to the kid and maybe do some good, or do you want me to rant?" You can only engage kids if you're genuinely interested in them. I don't mean interested in the problems they pose, but interested in their character, their opinions, their fears and frenzies, what makes them happy, what makes them individuals.

You see, in that way I'm lucky. I like people, I like kids, I like to hear what motivates them, what they love. It's bloody rare to come across a kid who is constituted of nothing but wickedness. They can be wicked, all right, but the evil is mixed in with some much more generous stuff. Down at the Hobsons Bay Hotel in Williamstown one time, I was chatting away with a group of blokes, including Hal Walker, an acquaintance. Hal kept a shop just across the road on the corner of Ferguson and Cecil, a takeaway place.

He was complaining bitterly about the local kids zooming up and down the footpath outside the shop on their skateboards, or leaving their bikes resting against his windows. Scared away customers, put the lives of other customers—older ones—in jeopardy. I asked Hal if he'd ever spoken to the kids, as opposed to screaming at them. He said the kids should know that what they were doing was wrong, without being told. I said I'd stop by one day and talk to them, which I did. And yeah, I talked to the kids in a sane way, pointed out that some of Hal's older customers weren't nimble enough to get out the way of a skateboard. The kids, every one of them, said: "Sorry, sorry". And they agreed to go further up the street to skate, a patch where there was no pedestrian traffic. I went back and told Hal at his shop that he wouldn't have to worry about the kids anymore. "Bloody hell, Les! You got those little bastards to listen to you." I said: "I did, Hal. You give it a try. They want to like you, they want to like everyone, pretty much. Give 'em a chance."

You can learn things from kids. I don't mean how to use your mobile phone in a fancy way, kids having so much more mastery of digital stuff than people of my generation. No, I mean that they can teach you about such things as courage, and daring, and joy. I've looked into the eyes of kids who've been belted from pillar to post by the circumstances of their lives, and I've seen raw defiance. Sure, a certain amount of anger has taken hold, but you know, in that defiance there's a message that says: "I'm going to have a life whatever it takes. I'm not going to be treated like shit." Now, these kids don't know how to bring the richness and happiness that's abroad in the world into their lives. But they haven't given up. I see courage in that defiance, and often enough I find myself saying: "Bloody hell. I don't know if I could find the grit these kids have got."

8

Gangland

Amongst street kids, homeless kids, disadvantaged kids, you don't come across too many lone wolf types who lead a gang of one on crime sprees. When kids are up against it, a tribal thing gets into them: they want companionship, and they form gangs. Most of the gangs I've encountered have protocols and rites that they hold sacred, and these rites hold them together, bond them. Because what they're looking for is a sense of belonging, and they don't belong to the broader, mainstream society around them. They want to feel special. And in a way, they want to show that they can be trustworthy, candid, reliable. But only to each other. In a gang, you might have a sense of right and wrong that goes further and deeper than amongst people outside the gang. You don't lag, for one thing. You don't dob in your mates. You share. You sympathise with other gang members who've suffered rotten bad luck. You stand up for your comrades. And all this time, you might, as a gang member, be doing all sorts of hair-raising shit, dealing, thieving, enforcing, menacing. Whatever you're doing, if you're in a gang then you're in a tribe, and that helps to hold everything together.

We've had gangs in Melbourne for as long as we've had Melbourne. Or at least, as long as we've had an underclass, which is from the beginning. In every era, gangs form to gain the advantage of numbers, which is an important consideration if you're about to hold up a stagecoach, rob a bank or set up a scam. And if you've got a gang, you'll need someone in charge if you're going to get anywhere. The boss is usually the bloke with a few more brains than anyone else; also a bit more ruthless. Ned was the standout in the Kelly Gang, far more intelligent than his brothers and his mates, and with a vision of what he wanted to accomplish, which was to become feared throughout the colony. Feared and admired.

Of course, it's only the gangs with violence in their culture that we ever talk about. If Ned had merely subjected the coppers to pulling faces at them and name-calling, we'd barely have heard of him. It's the bullet through the brainbox that captures our attention. Street gangs relish being considered outside the rules of society, and nothing makes you more of an outsider than murder. But you have to remember that there are also white-collar gangs, groups that conspire to stuff their pockets with money that really belongs to someone else, without ever picking up a pistol. In our own time, we saw how gangs of conspirators managed to drain the public of billions of dollars during the GFC, back in 2008. These guys made secret agreements, recognised certain leaders, acted knowingly against the laws of the land, and pretty much got away with it. The white-collar gangs, by never relying on murder as a protocol of their operations, have far, far greater success than the armed gangs. But you're not about to get into a white-collar gang without a white-collar education. That rules out all the clients I deal with.

No, the thing is that a bullet in the brainbox means more to the general public than any number of secret agreements by men in expensive suits. Murder is charismatic. Cooking the books is not charismatic. The Misters and Missuses of the general public shriek: "Murder! That could happen to me! Catch those villains and lock 'em up!" The Misters and Missuses never think: "Conspiracy between ex-private school kids! That could happen to me!"

So it's the gangs who opt for violence that I've dealt with; not the boardroom gangs. My experience of these gangs goes right back to my boyhood in Braybrook when the Footscray Boys and the Balmoral Boys (named for Balmoral Street in Footscray) were forming. I think my first encounter was a time when I hopped off a bus somewhere in Braybrook right into a nest of Footscray Boys. What age was I? Twelve? Thirteen? I was tough and I could look after myself, sure, but these boys were older and tougher. I may have given a bit of cheek to one or more of the gang members earlier in the day—can't be sure, but it sounds like me—and they recognised me when I jumped down from the bus. One of them said: "Him, that little shit, whack him!" A bottle was hurled that hit me on the noggin. I took off and didn't stop until I reached our house. My brother, Gary, was hanging around about the front of the house, and I shouted at him to help me.

"With what?" he said.

I looked behind me, and yeah, no one in sight. Funny how you can be running for your life from a gang of bad boys and still hear their footfalls behind you even when they're not there.

Just living in Braybrook in the 1950s and 1960s made you a target of the gangs if you were a boy of a certain age. The Footscray Boys hated me simply because I wasn't one of them. They hated any Braybrook kid, any Sunshine kid who gave the impression of having an independent spirit. Being chased at the bus stop was only one of a half dozen times I had to run for my life from the Footscray Boys, the Balmoral Boys. At the Royal Show another time, I had the Balmoral Boys bearing down on me, and again, at Hanging Rock, on a cricket club picnic, I was only saved from a hiding by the Footscray Boys when the other cricketers came to my rescue. It would be true to say that I copped more attention from the gangs than some other kids simply because I had a reputation as a tough little bugger. Not that I went about belting other kids; no, my rep came from my style of play on the footy field. Out there in the hurly burly of a match, I was diabolical, clouting opposing players left, right and centre. I was the designated assassin of our team, Sunshine YC, the kid other kids came to during the game. "Hey, Les, that number twenty-eight for Albion, he give me an elbow in the guts." Okay, off I go, locate number twenty-eight, belt him in the kisser, carry on with the match. Every footy side needs a first-class assassin or two. In the VFL, Collingwood had Murray Weideman and Des Tuddenham; Carlton had John Nicholls; Dermie Brereton filled the assassin's role at Hawthorn in the 1980s. So, yeah, a tough little bugger I was, but not off the footy field. I was just a mouth. And a cheeky one at that.

Now, the point I'm making is this: when you're in a gang, you're at war every day. Gang members don't take holidays. They're ready for conflict, ready to hand out retribution, ready to take by force what doesn't belong to them 24/7. They're in full-time employment, in other words. And once those gang members get used to this sort of employment—long periods of doing nothing, followed by brief periods of high-adrenalin biffo—they don't want a nine-to-five job. It's too tame.

That movie, *Romper Stomper*, with Russell Crowe. It came out in 1992, attracted big audiences. A neo-Nazi gang in Footscray at war with Vietnamese gangs. Ends badly for the male lead, Hando. The release of the movie marked a significant escalation in confrontations between the western suburbs' Vietnamese and skinhead gangs. Something I noticed after the movie's first couple of months in the cinemas was that the Vietnamese in Footscray started carrying knives. They felt more threatened than they had in the past. It wasn't that the movie spurred mass recruitments to Vietnamese and skinhead gangs; it was just that the film lent a type of squalid glamour to belonging to gangs. For the neo-Nazi boys, the movie made it seem that you could be both sexy, like Russell, and tough as nails. Now, most of the actual leaders of the neo-Nazi gangs were bloody ugly, bad teeth, acne scars, poor standards of hygiene. All of this, on top of being morons. But Russell, he wasn't ugly, and he had perfect teeth, and women loved him. For the Vietnamese, I think they liked the fact that in the movie, Asian guys didn't put up with any shit. I don't know whether you've noticed, reader, unless you were wandering about Braybrook and Footscray and Sunshine in the early '90s, but guys in gangs don't have that much imagination. It's not their forte, as the saying goes. So, they pick up style tips from movies. All those mafia movies, like *The Godfather* and *Goodfellas*, mafia guys loved them. Hoodlums like Sonny in *The Godfather*, sexy and violent and fearless, he must have become the model for a whole generation of mobsters. Hando in *Romper Stomper* became a model for the Footscray skinheads. And the Vietnamese modelled themselves on Tiger, the main Vietnamese character in the movie.

So, the gang stuff is coming more and more into my domain from 1992 onwards, and I can see the time ahead when gangs will become as big in my patch as they are in America, particularly in LA. I was worried, as you can imagine, and I stayed worried through 1993, all the way up to '96. I happened to be speaking about the whole business with Mick McCallum, a reporter from Channel 9, and Doug Ackerly, a terrific journalist and broadcaster and a good mate of mine. Little by little this plan emerged over a few weeks and a few dozen samples of the chilled article. Doug and I would fly to LA and get some footage and audio of the gangs in the east of the city, stuff that would make a story for current affairs on Channel 9, and might even make a bigger story linking into the growth of the gang problem in the west of Melbourne. I got a little bit of leave from Sunshine Council, on the understanding that this trip to the States would serve as research for local issues. All well and good, so Doug and I jet off to LA, intending to meet up with a cameraman whose name has been provided by Mick McCallum—as for sound, audio, Doug will handle that. Now, it will be evident to the reader that this whole escapade had a bit of a half-baked aspect to it, being that neither Doug nor I had any experience of LA. Well-intentioned, but half-arsed. But I did have a letter from the Victorian Chief Commissioner of Police, Neil Comrie, introducing me to the LAPD; very handy. Neil's been a mate ever since I brought him and Neil Mitchell from 3AW together at a restaurant in Chinatown to smoke the pipe of peace. The two Neils had been casting nasturtiums on each other's geraniums for a few years; not friendly at all, but after the Chinatown lunch, things were apples.

At LAX, the immigration folk wanted to know where Doug and I would be staying in LA. Not an unreasonable request. But we didn't know. We thought we'd get out of a taxi somewhere in downtown LA and book into a mid-range hotel, no problem. "Yeah," says the immigration guy behind the desk at LAX, "but which hotel?"

Which hotel? "Got any ideas, Doug?"

And in fact, Doug did have the name of a hotel; one that he'd stayed in on an earlier trip to LA; about a hundred years earlier. At that time, the hotel Doug wrote down on the arrival card, The Cecil, was indeed a mid-range venue of hospitality. But times must have changed because the immigration guy looked at the name and gave a huge snort.

"You must be kidding me. The Cecil? It's a flophouse. You guys don't want to go anywhere near it."

But Doug was adamant. "No, no, lovely place, salubrious accommodation."

The immigration guy called over a colleague. "What do you think? These guys are staying at The Cecil."

The second guy guffawed. "Good luck with that. You're Aussies, right? I thought you were civilised people."

Out at the taxi rank, none of the drivers could be persuaded to take us to The Cecil.

"No way, man. Not going nowhere near that place."

Finally, we found a driver who said he'd drop us off close by, but not at the door. Struggling along the footpath of this derelict neighbourhood, we were mugged twice. The first guy demanded money from Doug. Cool as a cucumber, Doug said: "Buddy, just off the plane from Australia. Haven't got a US cent on me." The guy waved him away, with contempt. The second guy, a little further down the footpath, chose me as his target. I said: "Mate, I'm just off the plane from Australia. No US dough." He gave me a whack on the head and hurried away. Doug was shaking his head. "That'll teach you to go telling lies, Leslie."

When we, finally, battled our way into the lobby of The Cecil, I have to say that the derision of the immigration guys and the caution of the taxi drivers was easier to understand. It was a dump. Everyone we saw, including the bloke at reception, gave the impression that he was armed and ready for anything, homicide in particular. The corridors echoed with screams. We glanced in through one open door and saw a guy in an advanced state of insanity rolling around on the floor. We had to barricade our door when we settled down for a sleep. Doug, nothing daunted, told me that I was being a sook. "Seen worse," he said. "Can't recall where, but I'm sure both of us have seen worse."

Had we seen worse? No. There wasn't a suburb in Australia that was as dangerous as that region of East LA. You have to be thankful that we in Australia have never had the easy access to firearms that Americans consider their constitutional right. Oh, boy. East LA, as we came to appreciate, was just by itself home to more owners of guns than all of the major Australian cities combined. And that's a big factor in gang recruitment. The LA gangsters, they've got their Walther P99s or their Beretta M9s tucked in their belts, and it gives them a feeling of power. They're never going to enjoy that feeling of power in any of the more conventional ways; never going to be elected to high office; never going to run a big business. But the Beretta in your belt—that's real power. In Australia, in a gang like the Footscray Boys, you could frisk a dozen kids and find a single pistol. The LA gangs are way ahead of our boys.

Now as it turns out, Doug and I chose a bad time to come to LA, because the whole city had just experienced the worst floods in decades. Doesn't flood that much in LA—doesn't even rain that much—but with our unerring talent for being in the wrong place at the wrong time, we'd come to the city while it was still drenched. Our contacts at the LAPD told us that we needed to go somewhere and chill for a week, let the flood waters drain away. Mexico was the suggested destination, Tijuana, just over the border from San Diego. Mexico in 1996 wasn't the dark fantasy world it is now, but it was on the way. Lots of spooky stuff going down in Tijuana, lots of good reasons not to go filming, or asking questions. So we didn't. We chilled. We drank tequila at cafes, watched the bad guys sauntering along the boulevards, studied the good guys selling nachos, drank more tequila. It's easy to get used to, chilling out with tequila in Tijuana.

After a week, back to LA, where we hired a Tarago and met up with the cameraman recommended to us. Then off to LAPD Central, showed the chief my letter from Neil Comrie. We were assigned to travel with the CRASH Squad. Fuckin' hell, there were a lot of bad guys down there in East LA who had no interest in being filmed for Australian television. I'd sidle up to a gang member, introduce myself as Les Twentyman from Down Under, mind if we film you as you go about your wicked business?

"Who you say?"

"Les Twentyman, Channel 9, Melbourne Australia. And this is my offsider, Dougie. Maybe some footage of you dealing crack?"

"Say what? I ain't dealing no crack. You know my message to Australia and Channel 9 and Dougie? Fuck off!"

Not cooperative. A bit overwrought. We tried one gang guy after another; nothing doing. Eventually we found a bad guy more talkative than his brothers and he let us wire him up for an interview. He spoke to us about the culture of the streets, problems with the cops (I don't think I'm breaking a confidence by saying that the bad guys and the cops didn't see eye-to-eye), good stuff for a Nine News at Six Special Report. But you know what struck me on this journey into the streets of East LA? Not many winners in the gangs. Kids with guns, sure, and heaps of gear traded, but being in a gang is not a good career choice. Most of the gang members are about the same age, late teens, early twenties. I'm thinking: "Limited life expectancy in gangland".

And right there, you have the issue. I don't think these kids care if they die on the streets. They're not looking ahead and thinking: "Hmm, another ten years, moving up the ladder, might become a lieutenant". According to the crime statistics, more than 20 percent of kids who get into a gang in LA at sixteen are dead in five years, while another 30 percent are serving a prison term. That's a much higher rate of fatalities than service in the US armed forces in a war zone. The whole gangland scene, you can only keep going if you think in the short term, because there is no long term. And that's exactly why we need the programs in Australia that give marginalised kids something that makes them think twice about getting into a gang and putting their brains on a short-term setting. Such as sport. More about that later.

Most of the gangs of the city are black or Hispanic. Down in East LA, they're black. No surprises there: black kids are more likely to grow up in poverty. And it's not just poverty that drives black kids into gangs; it's racism. White cops slag off African Americans every chance they get. Doug and I heard plenty of it. This was five years after the Rodney King bashing—the black guy, stopped in his car after a chase, had the living shit belted out of him by white cops, all captured on camera—and the wallopers were telling jokes about it. We were expected to join in the hilarity, Doug and I, but we just looked away, or at the ground. There'd been huge race riots in LA in 1992, sparked in part by the King beating, but I have to tell you, there's not much evidence of a change in the racist culture of the cops.

You have to be game if you're going to go looking for footage of the East LA gangs. I can be game. I can also be a sook, but when it comes to the work, I'm game. Doug and I were cruising in our vehicle looking for something to bring home on film this one day when I saw what looked like a gathering of gang members on the footpath down a narrow street. I said to Doug: "Brother, let's go". Doug was a bit tardy, but me, I was down there in ten seconds, in earnest conference with a guy who looked like he might be the leader, wanna get you on camera, whaddya say? He didn't say anything friendly after hearing the word 'camera'. He stuck the muzzle of a pistol in my face and told me to get the fuck out of the place. Which I did. We took off in the vehicle but after we'd put a little distance between Captain Hardarse and ourselves, we stopped when we saw a guy who looked pretty street savvy. I jumped out, gave him my spiel. "Yeah you can interview me, dude. But not here. Tell you why. You see that white Buick parked down there? Yesterday it did a drive-by, shot three guys." These days—2017—every news bulletin includes at least one story about Syria, the war there, explosions, executions. Well, down there in the streets of East LA, that's war, too. Armed gangs shooting the shit out of each other every day.

I came back to Australia wiser for the experience; wiser about the dynamics of gangs, at least. We'd sent the footage to Mark at Channel 9, so it had already been shown on the news by the time Doug and I returned. Follow-up interviews, all of that sort of thing. I was hungry for knowledge about street crime, and more especially about prevention; about the sort of programs that could help me help the kids. Over the years, I found sponsorship to get to the struggle streets of US cities in search of programs that could be applied in the west of Melbourne. So, I went to Ohio to study the unfolding of the gun buy-back scheme, and to Chicago and back to LA to get footage of the gangs in that city. It all helped me. Or it helped me when it wasn't likely to kill me. In LA another time, way down in Skid Row, I was filming with my own camera when two cops on motorcycles roared up and came to a halt beside me. One said: "You don't want to be going down that street with your camera on show. There are guys down there who'll take the camera then cut your balls off, you know." I told the cops I'd be apples, and headed into the Dark Zone. Halfway along, a posse of gang members emerged from a ramshackle building and demanded to know what the fuck I thought I was doing. I said: "I'm from Australia," as if that explained everything. It didn't, of course. It's possible to overrate the impression you're making by saying: "I'm an Aussie". The gang boys, they wanted to know my beeswax in the LA. One said: "You filming us, honky? You is, ain't you, you filming us, what the fuck?"

Me: "Filming you? No, no, no. Well, yes. Yes, I am. But it's for Australian television."

These guys could see the red light on my video camera and wanted to take a closer look. Now, if I'd handed over the camera—worth three thousand bucks—I'd never have seen it again. So, what was the best thing to do? Stand there debating the right of blokes like me to film black kids on the South Side? Or run? I chose the second option, zipped away in a manner that belied my fifty years and well-padded physique. The four gang guys chased me, and would, I think, have overtaken me and maybe shot me except that I turned at a corner and almost banged into a cop car stopped at an intersection. The cops looked at me, looked at the gang guys, stepped out of the car. The gang guys turned tail. One of the cops, a black guy, said to me: "Who you? What you doin' down here?" He meant, what is a white guy doing in the area at all.

"Oh, um, Officer, I'm Les Twentyman from Australia, filming these bad boys in my role as a youth worker." Something like that. The cop said: "Yeah? Well you be goin' back Down Under in a body bag if you hang round here, man. Get your arse somewhere safe." Which I did.

On another visit to the US, Chicago again, gathering material including footage for educational seminars back in Australia, I managed to persuade a gang member (was he in the Black Panthers? Or the Black Disciples?) to take me on a tour of the tough neighbourhoods. This guy and his girlfriend picked me up in his car, drove me to an estate where drugs and violence were big, big problems. We're not on the estate for long before we hear gunshots, whole volleys. My guy does a U-turn and is heading to safety when a whole posse of kids starts chasing the car, shouting their heads off. I think: "Bloody hell?" My guy says: "You a white dude, so they think you're a drug dealer, man. They wanna catch you and steal your shit. They don't find anything they can use, they kill you. Nice and bright—a Colombian necktie. Cut your throat for you from ear to ear, jerk your tongue out through the gash."

I've included these little episodes so that my readers are made aware that my life as a youth worker was not all banquets and speeches and fancy cars and glamorous women; there was some danger to the Twentyman life and the Twentyman limb. In fact, it's a wonder that the Twentyman life and limb have survived as long as they have.

There's another hazard in my line of work I must mention at this point. It's to do with meeting so many people in a job that's all about meeting people. My memory is pretty good for names and faces and where I've met so-and-so and under what circumstances. But I can't recall everyone. Back in 2000, I was off on a speaking tour that took in five European countries, mostly Scotland and Denmark. All well and good, but in the week before I left, I noticed that my ears were aching, off and on. Phoned the quack who said: "Here's your problem. Your ears are aching." Brilliant piece of medical diagnosis. He also said he couldn't do the fixing because he was too busy. "I'll book you in to see the locum," he said. "And Les, what about your prostate? Anyone had a gander at that lately?" Well, no. "Right. I'll get the locum to check your prostate, too." Got the earholes cleaned out by this lady locum, then it was time for the arsehole. Dropped me daks, a little reluctantly, was preparing to bend over when the lady locum said: "Mr Twentyman, there's something I must confess. Some years ago, you were my PE teacher at Mount St. Joseph's Secondary. Thought I should tell you." There was a reunion coming up for Saint Joe's kids, and I'd be attending. So would the lady locum. I rapidly pulled up my daks and said I'd come back another day for the prostate probe. And she smiled. Well, I mean, I couldn't give a speech to the assembled Old Girls knowing that one of them had handled me with rubber gloves a week or so earlier. Call me over-sensitive if you must, but there's no way that was going to happen.

9

Apex

The public is in a running sweat at the moment about the gangs dominated by Africans from Somalia, South Sudan, North Sudan. Australia has been accepting refugees and immigrants from those countries for some years now, and we have sizeable communities of Somalis and Sudanese living in Melbourne, mainly out west, Craigieburn, South Morang, Roxburgh Park, but also around Dandenong, Noble Park and Donvale. Mister and Missus Citizen are worried that the Africans won't assimilate and will carry on in Australia like the crazy Muslims they were in their birth countries—although many African refugees are actually Christians—and the people fleeing their homelands are trying to get as far away as possible from the murders and torture and atrocities that make up the day's news back in Somalia and Sudan. The truth is that Africans are not over-represented in the gangs of Greater Melbourne, but they do dominate one particular gang, the most notorious of all, the most bolshie, and that's Apex.

Apex got its start in Dandenong, and after a couple of years out there, has established itself as the baddest of the bad. Only about eighty fully fledged members, and maybe a couple of hundred more kids actually identify with the brand. Now, if you want to run a gang, you've got to have more on your agenda than making a bloody nuisance of yourself. Making a nuisance, it's not that hard. Smash a few windscreens with a crowbar, take a piss in public, slash a few tyres, throw up some graffiti on the wall of a Centrelink office. Kid stuff. If you want to get ahead, you have to graduate from petty crime to dealing. Drugs are not that hard to get your hands on, and it's a bloody big market. But here's the thing. If you want to start dealing in Melbourne you're going to get into conflict with the Big Boys—biker gangs mostly, people who gave up merely making a nuisance of themselves years ago and went into serious crime. The long-established dealers don't want amateur competition, and they make their views known.

Newbies like Apex, they see the lie of the land and accept an offer from the big boys. "You sell our gear out on the streets, you get a cut." The big boys don't want to get down and dirty on the streets. Hell, no. They've got clubhouses, pool tables, high quality booze laid on: Jim Beam, Southern

Comfort, Jack Daniels, Chivas. They want to be indoors trying to sink the black ball off the side cushion, watching *Game of Thrones* or listening to CDs. (You know who bikies enjoy from the old days? Tina Turner. 'Proud Mary'.) The last thing they care for is standing in the rain down at the corner of Stanley Street and Smith palming baggies of ice. So the kids in the gangs become the skanks of the big boys, all the dirty stuff. But here's the thing. We know how a gang evolves from amateur hour to the big stage. The Apex boys, they're going to think before long: "How come we're doing all the donkey work?" And they'll want to step up. Expect war.

Any way you look at it, the gang problem is growing. But at least the cops are now much more candid about the breadth of the whole thing, mainly thanks to Pat Boyle's scholarly work on the issue. I've been involved for long enough in all this stuff to get a grasp of the business. I met Paul Bray when he came to Melbourne a little while ago. Paul's a New Zealand copper, an expert on gangs in the Shaky Isles. They've got a huge Islander gang problem over there, also Maori gangs, Bikie gangs, white supremacists. We've got Islander gangs in Melbourne, and Paul was giving his insights to our local wallopers. One of the programs the Kiwis run is an Arts and Drama shindig, very effective; the kids are engaged in a way they wouldn't be if they were just being lectured to and scolded. And as I mentioned, we have our own Arts and Drama stuff running, just as promising as the NZ programs. I see it in the faces of the kids, absolutely. They come to me (I'm watching on) give me a high five, a knuckle tap. "Love this, Les." I'm thinking: "Okay, what is it that lights up these kids?" I think it's just a matter of using their creativity. Something about that, being creative, that trumps running around with a bowie knife or a Glock looking for strife. See, when you're in a gang, that's drama, that's a sort of low-level creativity. But if you can get the same buzz without risking a big, bleeding puncture in the skin that covers your guts, or a prison term, then you've had a win. Some of these kids might go on to make a living from acting. Could happen. Might sometime be taking myself and Cherie off to the MTC to enjoy one of these kids in the role of Macbeth, maybe one of the Sudanese kids playing Othello. I'd love that. If the society in which these kids live can make life seem something big and thrilling, the problem's gone. No kid at the age of sixteen, seventeen thinks to himself: "You know what I want to do more than anything in the world? I want to kill someone. I want to beat someone's brains in. I want to deal a thousand baggies of ice." What these kids hope for is to be thrilled, engaged, made to feel alive. Yeah, I know that everyone has to accept a bit of monotony. But you're not going to get through to any prospective gang member by saying: "Yeah, life's boring, get over it". What I want are programs that give kids a shot at life, at least. Just that.

I was up in Canberra last year to address the Federal Parliamentary Health Committee on the topics of ice, school suspensions and teen street gangs. If you're talking to a committee, you sit at the same table as the committee members, at this huge sheet of Australian cedar. Makes you feel like visiting royalty. And all the members question you politely. It's not an adversarial thing. I've got knowledge of what we're talking about; the members want to increase their knowledge. Me, I'm the only passionate bloke at the big table. The members care, sure, but it's another day at the office for them, mostly. I say I'm passionate, but I don't thump the table with my shoe and sound off at society. I just try and make my points, and make them clearly. The chairperson says: "Could you outline your views about the distribution of methamphetamines in our cities and towns, Mr Twentyman?" And I do. I tell the members that ice is flavour of the decade and the distribution is so well organised by various gangs that you can get what you need even in small towns all over the country. I give the members a few ice tales just to spook them into action. Then we move onto gangs, and school suspensions, which are skyrocketing, kids in the playground dealing in ice, gangs recruiting kids at school. What I try to impress on the members is that we're approaching the crest of a crime wave amongst young offenders. "What attracts these young people to crime, Mr Twentyman?" I'm asked, and I'm, you know, "Mate, it's not higher mathematics. You offer ice to a kid who wants a bit of action in his life, he's going to pay for it. Then he's going to want more, but his piggy bank is empty. So, he's reduced to the option of theft." And the members sigh and shake their heads. "What can be done in your view,

Mr Twentyman?" I tell them we need trained outreach workers in every school, and we need programs to back up what the outreach workers can offer. I'm talking about those art and drama programs, also sport, like my Redskins Basketball thing. We're not impotent, I tell the committee. We know the things that work. Then I say: "And we know what doesn't work, and that's more and more law and order. Law and order is the end of anything imaginative. Think about it. You hire more cops, you're just making the problem way too crude. It's like saying, 'See a head, kick it'. Kids want a life. We have to have the imagination to help them build something. Kicking heads is not giving kids a life."

10

Kill Your Rivals

It wasn't only the US that I relied on for knowledge of the gang culture. I went to the UK a couple of times to take notes about 'Youth at Risk' schemes being run over there. Whenever kids are said to be 'at risk' it's understood that what they're at risk of is getting into criminal gangs. Whenever disadvantaged kids adopt gangs, or are adopted by gangs, they become criminals. Kids don't form gangs that roam the city looking for opportunities to help old ladies cross the street. The culture of gangs is anti-social, because the point you're making by joining a gang is that you want to be seen by society as an outsider. People think that the big attraction for kids to join gangs is to make a fortune out of crime. You think? Crime—selling drugs, larceny, and so on—is not necessarily all that profitable. Oh sure, you stage a hold-up, you get away with twenty thousand, split it four ways, six ways, ten ways, take home maybe fifteen hundred bucks. Fifteen hundred bucks is two weeks' salary for many mid-range jobs; not that big a deal. Or your gang sells ice, rakes in twenty thousand a week, and an individual gang member might put a couple of thousand of that in his pocket for a year or two before he goes to prison for a term and earns nothing. It's not that crime doesn't pay; no, it's just that for most gang members, what it pays is rubbish over a five-year period. There was a study done in US jails of prisoners aged forty and above: dealers, corner guys. Many of the prisoners in the study, under conditions of anonymity, provided estimates of what they'd made from crime over their lifetimes. The great majority had earned less out of twenty, thirty, forty years of crime than if they'd worked behind the counter at Maccas for the same period. No, it's not the money that draws kids in, or not only money; it's the mystique and the status.

I went to Belfast and England in 1998 with my offsider, Mike, to take a look at the Youth at Risk programs being run there. I was no longer with Brimbank Council at that stage; I'd moved to Open Family—Father Bob's mob—of which more later, as they say. It was thought that the Youth at Risk programs could flourish in Australia, and I was keen to take a gander. Even before we left for the UK, I was warned in a very solid way to steer a mile clear of the politics of the city; the IRA versus the RUC,

Catholics versus Protestants business. I said: "Yeah, no worries".

Youth at Risk was a charity, with a certain amount of funding from the government and a lot of funding from sponsors, like Virgin. The YAR programs ran in communities, prisons, schools and universities. They were said to have had a fair bit of success, but what I wanted to know was whether they were suited to what we were dealing with in Melbourne. The overall aim of the YAR programs and what we were trying to achieve in our patch was the same: get kids involved in life. But in Belfast, where Mick and I arrived in February, before the Good Friday Agreement of April, the street-level gang culture was overshadowed in the Catholic regions of the city by the much bigger gang culture of the IRA. Catholic Belfast was ruled by the IRA, which enforced a catalogue of laws backed up by corporal punishment. Bad boys on the streets in Belfast were hauled before IRA enforcers and kneecapped; a bullet through the whole structure of the knee, walk with a limp for the rest of your days. More serious transgressions could earn you a double kneecapping, or even a six-pack—ankles, knees, elbows. You might get away with a slap across the chops, or a rap on the shins with an iron bar, depending on the mood of the enforcer. With the IRA as a self-appointed inquisition, you can be sure that the kids who joined gangs and got on the wrong side of the enforcers had to be damned serious about what they were doing.

Belfast itself—what can I say? It's not Paris. It's one of those cities that has never known a period of real prosperity. Melbourne, it was the richest city in the world at one time, the gold rush era, and some fabulous buildings were erected, boulevards laid out, trees planted, the botanic gardens established. Not in Belfast. It's grim, hardly any buildings above three storeys, and not one that radiates a feeling of confidence. In the Catholic areas, especially, you get the feeling that people have been living on potato peel their whole life. Nothing lively and joyful has ever played itself out in these Catholic areas. Well, how could it? The British have always had a blind spot when it comes to Ireland. Even amongst kids in England—kids who marched and raised their fists in the street to protest against the Vietnam War—there was no sense of an appalling injustice going down in Northern Ireland. Kids grow up in Belfast with their allegiance to their tribe—Catholic or Protestant—running in their blood. If a kid hears about the murder of some other kid from the tribe that's not his own and his response is to dance a little jig of joy, you know that something very bad is going down in the community. Anyway, the rivalry between the blithering Catholics and the blithering Protestants wasn't what I went to Belfast to investigate. But the truth is that what I *did* go to Belfast to investigate was overshadowed by the politics of Ireland every single day I was there. In Australia, the gangs that form pretty much have to invent a manifesto of enmity. The skinheads of the western suburbs have to manufacture grievances about the Vietnamese, for example. "They come over here and take our jobs, they speak ching-chong rubbish." That sort of bullshit. What they really mean is that they need an enemy, and the Vietnamese will do because they're Asian, which is to say, not white. But in Belfast, the enmity between Catholics and Protestants has a basis of true discrimination. When the Catholics say, "All the good jobs go to Proddies," they're not making it up. Over the centuries, the good jobs *have* gone to Protestants. Any argument in Belfast comes back to the politics of tribes. So, that became my particular task: to work around the sectarian struggle.

I'll give you an example of the strife we had to deal with, Mike and me. We went to a school to witness one of the Youth at Risk programs at work, then afterwards—by this time it was midday—we asked a local if he knew a pub where we might get a counter ale and a pint of Guinness. "Down there," he said, jerking a thumb in the direction of the Falls Road. Now, the Falls Road, as many of my readers will know, runs through West Belfast all the way to Andersonstown out in the 'burbs, which is to say, through the hard-core Catholic areas of the city. A bit further north you find Shankill Road, hard-core Protestant. Mike and I, off we go, nothing daunted. We find the pub, but it's shut. 12.30, slap in the middle of lunch hour, and it's shut. Bugger this! We stood there scratching our heads, a thirst on me like someone crawling out of the Sahara, when a bloke appeared and asked if we were attempting to enter the premises.

"Yeah, we are indeed attempting to enter the premises. Got a thirst on me that could prove fatal."

"You'll be pushing the button if you want to be on the inside."

"What button?"

Sure enough, there was a button, not all that obvious, and when our friend pushed it a camera descended, studied us, and a few seconds later the door opened. We thanked our friend, sauntered inside, very tense atmosphere, a few blokes at the bar, a few at a table at the back of the lounge watching us through narrowed eyes. Mike said to me out of the corner of his mouth: "Don't like the look of this, amigo. Let's get out of here."

I said: "Take it easy. We haven't done anything."

We order our sup, throw it down, not a word spoken. Mike has broken out in a running sweat. "Les," he whispers, "they're going to cut our flaming throats."

Then I saw a bloke I recognised amongst the group at the table—Billy McKee, one of the hard men of the IRA, knew him from watching the SBS doco, 'The Troubles'.

"Mike, that's Billy McKee, gotta go and say hello."

"Hello, my arse. You'll get us kneecapped!"

Excitable fellow, Mike. In any case, the matter was taken out of our hands because the blokes at the table had heard me and we were called over.

"You know me face, then?" said Billy.

"Damned right. Billy McKee. Pleased to meet you."

Lovely chat with Billy, for ten minutes or so before he had to leave. One of his mates said he'd introduce us to someone even more famous than Billy. "Would that suit you, then?" We piled into two cars outside, me, Mike, six IRA blokes. Mike was making his will, convinced we were going to be disappeared, and his conviction was only made more certain when we pulled up in a wrecker's yard somewhere in West Belfast. He foresaw the two of us being thrown into a car and compacted.

And who was the man we were meeting? Brian Kennan. Brian had served a twelve-year prison term at Long Kesh for his activities with the IRA (including organising assassinations) and was now deeply involved in the peace negotiations with the UK government. What a turnaround! I admired the courage and commitment of the man to his cause—the cause of reconciliation.

We were taken to a caravan down the back of the yard, not luxurious, shook hands, nattered away. Brian remained suspicious of my reason for being in Belfast, so I showed him my card as proof of my bona fides. But my card at that time was printed in the colours of the Mighty Scraggers—red, white and blue, also the colours of the Union Jack, reviled by the IRA. I thought: "Oops!" Brian sent a colleague off to check me out, and there was a hiatus in the chatter until the colleague returned. He'd phoned a contact in Melbourne and had been told that I was kosher. Brian relaxed, opened a bottle of Jameson's, poured freely.

Back in 1998, when I met Brian, there were three or more versions of the IRA—the Real IRA, the Provisional IRA, and the Official IRA, each of them with a different attitude towards the peace talks with the British. And then there was a fourth IRA, which was the street level organisation—the enforcers I spoke of before, guys who handed out punishments to kids. Everything I learnt about youth programs in Belfast was overshadowed by the role played by the street-level justice of the IRA guys. Back in Australia, a fifteen-year-old kid and his fellow gang members who hold up a 7-Eleven are thought to be candidates for intervention by a youth worker, such as me. I'll talk to the kid and his mates in remand, maybe, or in a juvenile detention centre, see what can be done to get them all back to school when they're released. In Belfast, it could easily be that the IRA gets to the kid first and inflicts a certain amount of mischief on his kneecaps. In these two approaches to juvenile crime, you can make out two distinct ambitions for the offender. The IRA approach is to inflict dreadful pain on the kid, make him reluctant to ever transgress again. The approach in my patch is to open a few doors, encourage the kid to walk through them, maybe return to school, maybe find a job. My ambition for the kid is optimistic. The Belfast ambition is profoundly pessimistic. And primitive. Three thousand years ago, the tribes of Ireland would have been taking the approach to transgressions that the IRA employs. So, bloody hell, we've got to do better.

I moved on from Ulster to England, checking out the Youth at Risk programs down in South London. The organisers were taking a whole mob of kids from a juvenile prison up to the Lake District for ten days. Most of the kids were members of the Sutton Boys Posse, a gang that had been creating merry hell in the borough of Sutton for a few years. The Youth at Risk people had wrung an agreement from the kids to take part in the camp and had convoyed thirty or more of them up to a site in Wordsworth country. I was introduced to the kids as a youth worker from Australia, and was immediately honoured with the nickname, 'Skippy'. Now, I could tell from my first meeting with the kids that the organisers were maybe a bit too ambitious in hoping that the Sutton Boys would undergo some radical conversion of the soul just by being exposed to the glorious scenery of the Lake District. They were tough little buggers, these kids, and their engagement with the world was completely conditioned by their gang membership. What I mean is the kids didn't think: "Okay, I'm going to be a bad boy for a couple of years then settle down and adopt the laws and customs of English society". No, this was it, the gang, this was the dominating thing in their lives. They were genuinely proud of being Sutton Boys. When they were heading away from a break-and-enter in Sutton, they'd leave a business card behind in the house advertising themselves: 'Sutton Boys been here.'

But, sure, I tag along, make my notes, chat with the organisers and sometimes with the kids. Up at the campsite, a riot erupted on the first day, just outside the canteen before lunch. No idea what sparked it. Fists were flying everywhere; kids in strangleholds; others sinking the slipper into the tender bits of other kids on the ground. The Youth at Risk staff were struggling to break it up, save someone from death by boot and club. I was what might have been considered an honorary staff member so I jumped in and attempted to pull the kids apart, managing to wrestle one kid to the ground, with him alternatively head-butting me and sinking his choppers into my arm. I finally prevailed—me, at the age of fifty, for God's sake—looked into his blue eyes and suggested that he was taking any protests about the food just a tiny bit too far. The gang leader was standing close by and let out a great hoot of laughter. Oh yeah, that's me, that's Les, face bleeding, bruised and battered, still making jokes—which could be my undoing one of these days. But I didn't feel all that wise. I felt like an aging youth worker who should've got the hell out of the way.

And that wasn't the only fight over the ten days. These kids loved fighting—it was wholesome recreation to them. A couple of them jumped me one morning and somehow forced an iron bar up under my chin, pulling it tight enough to throttle me. My feet were dangling in the air, and my chaotic life flashed before my eyes. Then the Sutton Boys' leader hurried over and told the other two Suttons to let me go. "You don't want to go strangling Skippy. He's the only bloke here who knows arseways from Wednesday." Drawing in lungfuls of air, doubled over as I was, the Sutton boss patted me on the shoulder, "Sorry 'bout that, Skippy. My two must have had a rush of blood to the head." By the final day of the camp, I was exhausted in body and soul.

We didn't learn much from the Youth at Risk programs in Ulster and England about strategies to limit the influence of gangs. In my opinion, we were already doing better things on my patch. But I did learn this, and applied it to our gang situation: torture works, but at a hell of a cost. Kneecapping is torture. A whack across the shins with a crowbar is torture. Sure, the victim might think: "Not going through that again," and steer clear of larceny. But he's not going to embrace a more productive life, is he? He's marked for life, and his pessimism about the society around him is going to deepen. Okay, in Australia we don't have paramilitary organisations going about with missions to maim. But we have another version of it, called incarceration, locking kids up; it's not quite as primitive as a crowbar across the shins, but just as unlikely to achieve anything good. In my patch, I get heartburn whenever I hear politicians calling for mandatory sentencing for juvenile offenders, and more cops making more arrests. What I want are programs that make kids think of membership in a gang as a poor alternative. It's not rocket science. Open doors for kids, and a good number will walk on through.

11

Here Come the Redskins

Now, the doors. As I was saying, the door that most attracted the kids on my patch was the one that led to involvement in sports. I've taken the trouble in these pages to make readers aware that I was a pretty flash sporting figure in my youth—in Aussie rules, I might have gone on to win two or three Brownlows if I hadn't buggered my leg. And not just footy. Had a nice turn of speed, too; easy to imagine me on the top step of the dais having an Olympic gold medal slung around my neck. (Allow me a fantasy or two, reader, if that's okay.) It wasn't in the stars. I was a rascal of a rare sort back in those days; probably headed for a lifetime of mischief, but I found footy and it made the world of difference. It calmed me down. I don't mean just that sport was an outlet for my energy; it was more than that.

Sport is actually a creative thing. The sort of judgements you make out on the sports field can sometimes achieve a type of beauty which must be something like what a painter enjoys when he or she puts something on a canvas that feels as if it came from the gods. Watch the Gary Abletts playing, Senior and Junior. That's not just footy; that's art. Or Cyril Rioli. Now it's true that the Abletts and Cyril are the Michelangelos of our game, but even a mug player at times experiences moments of grace and daring that elevates him, her, to the heavens. When I was sixteen and captaining Albion Footy Club, I knew that feeling, and it was expressing my creativity—not simply burning up excess energy, that thrilled me in the way it did. And that's what I wanted for the kids I had in my care. So in 1998, working at this time for Open Family, I got a basketball team going out at the Maribyrnong Sports Centre with the help of Jim Markovski, another youth worker, top bloke, and Richard Tregear, a youth worker who specialised in working with Asian youth at risk, if I can put it that way. I'd coached basketball in schools and I knew it was the sort of game these kids could enjoy: everyone on a team got to handle the ball; almost every player had chances to shoot for goal; not much scope for biffo—too fast. I nudged my kids in the direction of the game, and they relished the opportunity.

The first team we formed we called the Redskins. They didn't have any uniforms at first. Didn't always have a ball, either, which you'll have to concede is a bit of an impediment to playing the game. I spoke to Bob Hart, who wrote a column headed, 'The Eye' for the *Herald Sun*, a free-ranging spray of journalism that took in the disadvantaged and their troubles. And in the way these things sometimes work out, that column was seen by Clive Smith, once the head of Deutsche Bank in Australia, by this time semi-retired and ready to give himself to philanthropy. Clive got himself in touch with me, asked me what we most needed. "A couple of basketballs would be good," I said. "Maybe uniforms for the kids. Footwear." Clive said: "Done".

The kids notice when people take trouble for them. The Redskins started off with next to nothing, and that's what these kids were used to—next to nothing. They don't necessarily expect things to improve, and when they do—when they see new basketballs, uniforms, footwear—it changes their mindset. A certain amount of optimism comes to life in them, simply because people who could easily have ignored them paid attention; showed some goodwill. Now, you can pay attention in various ways, maybe by inviting kids along to listen to sermons and self-improvement lectures, and if you did that you'd never see that optimism come into their faces. They'd think: "Same old, same old—do me a favour". But because it's basketball, they think: "Yeah!" And whenever possible, we try to provide a little extra delight by inviting sporting heroes along to meet the kids. No bigger hero in the sporting world than Muhammad Ali, right? Right. On one of his visits to Australia and to

Melbourne, Jeanie Pratt invited me to bring some kids along to meet the great man. I had this little live-wire in one of the teams, a certain Mohammad, and I'd promised this kid that one day I'd get him to shake hands with Ali if he stuck with the program. And so, on this day, I was in a position to say to Ali: "Muhammad, meet Mohammad." Over the moon, that kid was.

When we started up the basketball program in 1998, the population of Australia was 18.7 million, and in Melbourne, 2.3 million. And now, 2017, the Australian population is 24.3 million and Melbourne's population is 4.5 million. Over that nineteen-year period, tens of thousands of people from countries at war have settled in Greater Melbourne, a majority in the western suburbs. Which is to say, there are many more people out west whose journeys through life have been badly disrupted. Migrants bring to Australia gifts of resilience and enterprise, sure, but they also bring experiences of trauma. You're bound to get more to deal with when you take in the traumatised than if you're giving a home to Ten Pound Poms (as an example) from the dozy cities and suburbs of blithering old England.

The Somali civil war broke out in 1990, and in the west of Melbourne we took in some thousands of refugees from the Horn of Africa. The Sudanese civil war began in 1983, and by the mid 1990s, Sudanese refugees and migrants were flowing into western Melbourne, from Flemington out to Craigieburn. Whole families, or not quite whole; the dad was often missing, confirmed dead, presumed dead, or in a camp. The kids of these families—many of them—had seen things you wouldn't find in your worst nightmare. And being black, they were considered a bit iffy by the broader, predominantly white community. It's a bloody rare sort of person who has no desire to belong anywhere, and these kids from the wars wanted that security of belonging. They supported each other. Some of them formed gangs. And these new gangs had the same purpose and the same priorities of many of the existing gangs—white, middle-eastern, Asian, islander: stand proud, take no shit, identify your enemies, clobber them, fashion a source of income (drugs), get yourself a gun.

What I'd seen in East LA on my various visits made me sick at heart, because I could see it happening in Melbourne, in particular out west. I'm still sick at heart. Open Family, The Twentieth Man —what we've achieved with the Redskins—all of it could be overwhelmed by the influence of gangs. Let me give you the names of a few of the gangs that currently thrive in Melbourne's suburbs. SNK (St. Albans Kings Park); Apex (named after the street in Broadmeadows in which the gang first formed); KYR (Kill Your Rivals); 3LK (Love Liberty Loyalty Knowledge); Sunshine Boys. Up in Sydney, Brothers For Life is one of the better known gangs, now split into cliques, one of them exclusively Muslim. Gangs that keep going for a few years (and of all the gangs that start up, only about one in ten hangs on for more than a few months) not only develop their own culture, but that culture evolves, and gets a stronger hold on members. The gang becomes the country that the members live in. And in the same way that real countries feel the need to give themselves greater status on the international stage, so the gangs have to let you know that they exist, and are (as they say) 'a force to be reckoned with'. We haven't yet seen a full-scale, to-the-death war between street gangs in Melbourne—the sort of conflict that leaves a dozen bodies in its wake—but we will. We've seen wars amongst bikie gangs, sure, but a bikie gang is not a street gang. And amongst criminal gangs, the 'underbelly' gangs, yes, but criminal gangs are not street gangs either.

One of the problems we face back in Melbourne is the reluctance of the police to concede that gangs exist, or that they pose much of a threat. The evidence is there, but the cops, over the years, sort of shrug it away. I've wondered why that is and I think I know. You see, a gang is an organisation dedicated in its activities to making a mess of everything the cops uphold. Individual criminals, thieves, swindlers, blokes who rely on biffo to get their way, rapists, hoons—they're not part of an organisation; they're just everyday bad guys and thugs. And that's what cops can better comprehend—morons and thugs acting out of greed or malice. But if you have a gang on your patch, it's an expression of defiance. It's as if these gangs are saying: "Cops? Who cares?" So why grant them the reward of recognition? Because that's what the gangs want—recognition. They don't want to belong to a secret society; they want the members of the general public to quake in their boots at the mention of Kill Your Rivals. In an important way, public recognition is one of the main aims of gangs. Like the Sutton Boys I spoke of earlier, leaving calling cards at places they'd done over. We're here, we're lethal, you better fear us—that's the unspoken motto of every street gang. And it's something that distinguishes the street gang from other gangs. If you're in the Mafia in Melbourne, you're not about to shout it from the rooftops. No, no. Somebody from the media approaches you and asks you if you're the Mafia Don of Melbourne, you say: "Mafia? What Mafia? It doesn't exist". Think of that escapade last year of the Apex boys in the city, running amok down Swanston Street, knocking over seats at footpath cafes, howling like timber wolves. That's behaviour that's meant to draw attention to the gang. And that's why the cops are a bit coy about street gangs. Set up a gang, and it's an insult to the entire police force. My mate, Pat Boyle, a Detective Superintendent with Victoria Police, recently took a sabbatical to write a study of gangs—an outstanding piece of work. He's one of the few coppers who's prepared to acknowledge the problem. And amongst his conclusions is that the growing issue of violent street gangs is a consequence of their being ignored by law enforcement agencies for so long.

I harp away at intervention as a worthwhile strategy to combat the influence of street gangs because good, imaginative intervention works. Look at the people who are attracted to gangs. They're not in their eighties, getting about on Zimmer frames with clubs and guns and knocking over servos. They're not in their fifties, either; not in their forties, nor their thirties. They're kids. They've got tonnes of energy. And they don't see any way of using that energy. We might say: "Get an education, work hard, find a job, save your pennies, team up with a nice girl, get married, raise a family". Which is to say: become a law-abiding citizen. But these kids are what I call socially-excluded; they've developed a grudge against society because society has offered them so little: crap housing or no housing and a fraught path to employment. They've been ridiculed—many of them—because of their colour, or their faith, or both. Tonnes of energy, as I say, but no interest in using it creatively; using it to build. The feelings these kids have of exclusion—no stake in the society around them—can begin early. In one school out west, there was a hell of a problem with a marauding gang that went about bashing kids and what have you; and the gang leader, when he was identified, was a kid in Year 10—which is to say fifteen years old. The principal had him up to his office, told him he was expelled, and the kid, on the way out the door, abruptly spun around and whack!—knocked the principal out cold. Another kid of fifteen I was working with told me with a type of bravado that he'd stabbed another kid for twenty cents. Where does that bravado come from? From the need to shock, as if to say: "Oh, I'm a bad boy of a rare and frightful sort. You want to be wary of me."

    I had a couple of kids tell me in a jaunty way that carrying a knife out in the suburbs they hailed from was no big deal, just like carrying a mobile phone. Then I was involved in the case of eight kids, none over the age of fourteen, who'd filled their leisure time by plundering shops and homes, armed with baseball bats and sundry other weapons of assault. And another kid, fifteen, was finding it difficult to acquire a genuine pistol so he manufactured one himself by attaching a short length of brass piping to a wooden gun, then rigging a trigger that could fire a meat skewer from the barrel. Very proud of it, he was. (An incidental point: I made a bit of a thing of the pipe weapon outside a gun exhibition at Camberwell Town Hall, showing the media folk how it worked, thinking it might be appreciated by the public that gun exhibitions glamourised pistols. A bloke from the backers of the exhibition, the Shooters Association, wanted me arrested for having a pistol in my possession without a licence. I was leaving the Governor's Mansion in the Botanical Gardens following afternoon tea with the Governor himself when the police phoned me and wanted to have a chat based on the complaint. I could have passed from the Governor of Victoria into the care of the Governor of Port Phillip Prison, but it came to nothing.)

Now, we've got lots of citizens who have next to no sympathy for kids like those I've mentioned. The easiest thing in the world is to shout out: "Lock 'em up! Better still, send 'em all back to Africa! If this country doesn't suit 'em, they can go to buggery." Tabloid journalists—print and television and radio—think of opportunities to come down like a tonne of bricks on these kids, as their bread and butter. They salivate at the prospect of the editorials they'll write. And the journalists know what they're doing, because the public loves it. Now and again, in a gloomy mood, I reflect that public hangings or televised torture would grab a huge audience in our peace-loving society. But feeding the worst appetites of the public is not what gives us the culture we treasure; the laws that we honour. You can have a lynch mob, or you can have well-conceived laws that deal with bad guys in a humane way, whatever the crime. I know which of those alternatives I'd choose.

12

Sydney Town

I'm a very ambitious man. I haven't ruled out serving as Secretary General of the United Nations, and I think I'm good for the Nobel Peace Prize in a year or two. I also intend to be a person who owns three pairs of shoes at the one time, instead of the two pairs that tide me over at present. And I'd like to see the Les Twentyman Foundation go national, international, cosmic. As a modest first step on the path to glory, I've been up to Sydney a number of times over the past few decades to check out the lay of the land. My most recent foray was in 2014 when we had most of our ducks in a row for the launch of the LTF in the Harbour City. That good man, Chris Smith of 2GB, had been providing a spot for us on his show and I intended to make the announcement in the 2GB studios at Claremont, Lauren Jackson and Austin Blake on hand to attract attention. We had cleared a dozen hurdles on the way to NSW accreditation then, just as we were set to breast the tape, another hurdle popped up. If we were granted accreditation in NSW, that would mean that we were officially a national organisation, and we'd need to apply for accreditation again in Victoria. Bloody hell. So, we were compelled to put the Sydney launch on hold.

We'd made earlier attempts to get some runs on the board in Sydney, most of them problematical, I have to say. I was up in Kings Cross with a cameraman recording footage of gang members loitering about, palming little baggies of smack to customers. A very fraught business, filming these guys going about their work. The gang members who noticed my cameraman, caught my attention, did the finger across the throat sign, or made a pistol with their fingers and aimed at me. You might think: "Oh, yeah, pretending to be tough guys". But as I knew, and as the cops knew, these Sydney gangsters ran groups of dealers, five or six kids, with a good percentage of girls on the game. Any strife with the kids, the gang guys got rid of them: bullet in the back of the head, body disposed of quietly. The kids doing the dealing were homeless, many of them runaways. Nobody was going to miss them. But this time up in Kings Cross, a girl who was keeping out of camera shot came up to me after we'd gathered our footage and shyly introduced herself. "Mr Twentyman? Maybe you don't remember me,

Les's mother, Ilma, with the one-year-old Les (1949).

Les, playing Honey Bun, in the Braybrook High School production of *South Pacific* (1965).

Williamstown Under 19s Football team (1966) captained by Les, front row, 2nd from left. Middle row: far right, Sergio Beni, now Pres. Colac Rotary Club, great supporters of LTF; 3rd from right, my brother Garry; and 5th from right, Mike Good.

Captain and coach of Albion Reserves in 1975, Les is in front row, centre, holding a football. Second row from top, centre, vice-captain John Hyett who later became Mayor of Sunshine, now member of LTF board.

Yarraville Reserves coach, Les Twentyman, exhorting the men at three-quarter time during the 1977 grand final against Sunshine. In the last quarter, Yarraville came from behind and won the premiership convincingly.

Kevin Hillier (*Kevin and the D Generation*) with Les, at the 1987 20th Man Fund Christmas Party, Newport Junction Hotel.

A great supporter of the project, Premier Jeff Kennett AC and Les at the opening of the Smorgon 20th Man Fund crisis accommodation for homeless kids (1994).

Les and an Australian cameraman with LAPD officers from the CRASH Squad (Community Resources Against Street Hoodlums) during his visit to Los Angeles researching street gangs (1996).

Les and well-known restauranteur, Ian Hewitson, patron of the 20th Man. They raised $50,000 by being sponsored to lose weight – $1,000 for every kilo lost by them over 2 months (1998).

Les with test cricketer, Colin Miller, in MacNab Park in Footscray, talking to a boy who was injecting into his toes, having run out of veins elsewhere to inject into (1998).

Cherie and Les's wedding, Footscray Gardens (2006).

Les introducing the Dalai Lama at an event in Maddern Square, Footscray in 2010 where he pledged $100,000 to the 20th Man Fund (2013).

Brighton Rotary Sports Night LTF fundraiser. From left, LTF Chairman David Young, Les, centre front; behind him, Le Pines Funerals Vic. GM, John Fowler with staff; and Australian basketball champion Lauren Jackson (2016).

Luncheon to mark the name change from 20th Man Fund to the Les Twentyman Foundation. From left: Leigh Matthews, fmr AFL champion, LFT ambassador and Les, actor and LTF ambassador Gary Sweet, LTF chairman David Young (2016).

Brighton Rotarians Ian Mence, far left, and Paul Nicholson, with Les and former Redskins Basketballer and 20th Man Leadership graduate, Jasmine Garner, at the Night of Stars fundraiser. Jasmine was the first woman to kick a goal in the AFLW and is an LTF ambassador.

Dec. 2016: Les accepting a cheque from his granddaughter, Lotus, who instigated a student fundraiser at her school – Footscray West Primary School – for the LTF's Back to School program after fire burnt thousands of textbooks in the LTF warehouse just before Christmas 2016.

but I'm Jodi and you gave me my first-ever Christmas present when I was a little kid in Footscray. First-ever. And you took me to the tennis. D'you remember now?" I did remember. She'd been a sweet kid, Jodi, doing it tough. Her mother's name was Margaret, on the game down in Melbourne. And Jodi was on the game in Sydney.

That's the gut-wrenching thing to me, knowing that the most reliable predictor of a girl getting on the gear when she grows up, or going on the game, nearly always both, is the example she's set in the home. Mum's in bed with customers, day and night, that's what the daughter takes on a few years later. Mum's got a strap pulled tight around her upper arm, syringe in the other hand, that's what the daughter does when the blues are too bad to bear. Or maybe it's dad who's the problem, coaxing the daughter into bed, or mum's customers might be doing the coaxing. Anything we can do for these girls can be undone in one day of wretched abuse.

I told Jodi that I was up in Sydney at least once a month; told her where I stayed. "You come and see me, Jodi. Anything you need to talk through, I'll listen." She came, sure enough. Those visits and chats were all down to that Christmas pressie years ago, and it wasn't that Jodi thought there was any chance that she'd change her life just from yarning with old Les. I didn't want anything from Jodi, not even a concession that what she was doing out on the streets would probably end up getting her killed. A girl like Jodi, that beautiful and a prostitute, she wouldn't come across many men at all who wanted nothing from her. I was a bit of relief in her life of hire. Oh, and that tennis game. It was an exhibition match between Yannick Noah and Boris Becker before the Australian Open back in 1996. When this exhibition match was first proposed, the idea was that a whole lot of well-heeled establishment people would be invited along. But Boris, he said no. He wanted homeless kids, disadvantaged kids in there at the Tennis Centre, Melbourne Park. The organisers thought of me and my kids; invited us along. And I invited Jodi. She loved it.

We did manage to get a sort of mini launch up in Sydney, with Chris Smith as MC interviewing DS Deb Wallace, who spoke about gangs, mentioning that one gang member had told her that all of her colleagues in the police were so dumb for getting millions spent on CCTV cameras without building a single basketball court. One of the points she was making is that you get any amount of money for flash technology, but a humble place where kids can play—no, nobody understands what good that would do. Mind you, Deb told a story of eventually getting a couple of teams going made up of members of Asian gangs, then having to get members of both teams to bow before the start of play just to make sure the kids didn't have machetes down their shorts. Apart from Deb—a wonderful woman—we had Lauren Jackson up on stage, also Blake Austin, Mark Geyer, Kevin Sheedy, and that man with a great big heart, David Young.

You can't be in Sydney as many times as I've been, without pigging out at Doyle's on Watson's Bay—world-famous for its seafood. I was out there with Pip Mologousis, a mate I'd first met years earlier playing cricket for Williamstown; Pip was playing for Newport. Richard Lenarduzzi was with us that day, also Dennis Galimberti, who revealed that his parents came from the same village in Tuscany as Richard's. We were discussing LTF stuff, but I had this concern about the cost of the meal, Doyle's being notoriously expensive. I was discussing the homeless, and eating like the homeless, back in Melbourne—could barely afford a couple of chips and half a small prawn. Pip, now a successful businessman, says: "Mate, eat up, it's on me". He also got me to wager a small sum on a horse he had running that day—kept a few neddies, Pip did. I might even have won a few bob on Pip's nag. I tell this Sydney story to demonstrate the difference between a professional get-together in Sydney and one in my patch in Melbourne. If I was meeting people professionally in Footscray, we would have gone to a fish-and-chips joint on Barkly Street and fed ourselves for five bucks each. In Sydney, it's always considered that a business meeting has to have a bit of luxe about it. They're a more hedonistic mob up there in Sin City. You could be discussing an outbreak of bubonic plague and if the meeting was in Sydney, someone would say: "Listen, it's a bit gloomy, this plague thing. Let's have the discussion out at Doyle's just to lighten the mood a little."

It was in Sydney that ABC Stateline interviewed me on the subject of 'pauper graves', which is to say the burials of kids who have died in the care of the DOC (Department of Children). These kids die from overdoses, violent confrontations with each other or with pimps and customers (girls on the game, and most above a certain age are on the game), sometimes malnutrition. But the most common way in which these kids in care die is at their own hands—suicide, any of a half-dozen methods, including hanging. And it can happen that a number will die in a week, in which case the authorities save money by burying them in a mass grave. Isn't that just great? The kids spend their whole lives treated as rubbish, and in death, they're buried in a way that denies them any individuality. I've attended the funerals of any number of these kids, and I can tell you, it's a heart-breaking business to stand at a graveside with as few as one other person and watch that coffin descend.

The ABC interview was my second for the morning. I'd been on 2GB with Chris Smith earlier. And, you know, not feeling all that flash after the second interview. I thought: "Les, this could be serious, stroke, whatever, get yourself over to St Vincent's hospital". The doctors at St. Vinnie's carried out some tests and told me that not enough oxygen was reaching my blood. I thought: "Fucking hell, I'm breathing in oxygen so where's it going?" They put me to bed, bit of medication, but in the night the mayhem cases started arriving: stabbings, blokes going berserk on speed or whatever, one bloke who'd broken his leg by kicking the bejesus out of a wall in a police cell. I was moved to an armchair. Dozed off for a bit but was awoken by the sprinklers going off—an involuntary cold shower. After five in the morning by this stage. A nurse told me I'd be better off in my hotel room, so away I shuffled. Anything in the medical way that befalls me is never simple. Could have had a headache, bit of a pain in the tummy, but no, it has to be this oxygen thing, followed by eviction from my bed, followed by a sprinkler attack.

I have to admit it—Sydney has been a city of misadventures for the Twentyman carcass. The reason I was up in the Harbour City was to attend a gang forum out in Cabramatta. That was with our Open Family mob. I was still coping with oxygen deprivation on the first day of the forum and still on medication. But showing my usual bravado mixed with my usual stupidity, after hours of talking and listening, I thought it best to settle everything down at the hotel I was booked into—the Crest in Kings Cross—with a few glasses of vintage, red and robust. Then jumped into bed naked after scoffing a handful of pills. A few hours later my bladder was as tight as a drum and I slipped out of bed to attend to the necessary. I was in my birthday suit and in a disorientated state, thinking I was home I turned left instead of right, opened the door to the room and wandered out into the corridor. Hear that slamming sound? That's the door to my room closing behind me. Les, you moron, what's to do? I opened a cupboard and saw a whole heap of fire equipment and an emergency telephone. I picked it up and even in my addled state, realised it was dead. Also in the cupboard, a glass box: 'Break only in an emergency'.

If this wasn't an emergency, what the hll was? Broke the glass. A siren began blaring, and a voice announced over a loudspeaker that everyone in the hotel was as good as dead, pretty much. From inside the cupboard, I heard people running for the stairwell, screaming hysterically. I covered my delicate bits with a rubbish bin lid. After a few minutes of mayhem, a security guard swung open the door of the cupboard and looked at me in alarm. I explained the situation, and the guard nodded his head. "Don't worry, don't worry, happens all the time." He opened my room for me, and I scurried in, still shielding myself with the dustbin lid. You can see what I'm getting at, can't you? I'm out searching for people who need to be saved from themselves, when the fact is that I need to be saved from myself on a weekly basis. Tragic.

Well, we still haven't got the LTF up and running in Sydney. The most recent attempt was in Blacktown in 2014. So, I can't yet call for the LTF to be rebranded as Les Twentyman Foundation Worldwide and Universal Pty Ltd. That will have to be a task for the next generation at LTF. But seriously folks, what a good thing it would be if we could get our programs into every capital city. Because we're good at it, I have to tell you. We've been doing our stuff for so long now that we've got it down pat.

13

Father Bob

Now, Father Bob. I knew him well before I went to work for his Open Family mob. He'd been out there for years, rounding up the homeless, the abused, the bewildered—a good shepherd, yeah, but not above giving voice to a few choice words not found in the Holy Book. Bob's what you want to find in every priest—if only—a bloody big heart, a big brain, and the ability to sniff out bullshit. And the sniffing out, that's an important part of Bob's work and an important part of mine because you've always got people with brilliant ideas to sell you that benefit them more than the clients. "Oh, Father Bob, listen to this: we can gather up all these hopeless cases and sell them to a pet food company, invest the profits in a big, glossy booklet for the public. Leave it to me."

So, Father Bob and I met up frequently in the course of our work, took a shine to each other and shared the occasional glass of beer. It had never occurred to me that I might go and settle in Open Family. But then in 1997, thereabouts, the newly created Brimbank Council decided it could do with fewer youth workers, next to none, in fact, which left eight of us wondering what we'd do for a crust. We went through the usual rigmarole with an employer that had decided to shaft the staff. You know how it goes? "We have no plans to retrench our youth workers. None whatsoever. Whoever told you that is telling porky pies." A couple of weeks later: "Okay, maybe we have looked at the possibility of getting rid of a youth worker. No more than one. Or two. Could be four. Or five. Or eight." This was in the Golden Age of Outsourcing, an innovation that had enormous appeal to CEOs. Saves money. You outsource, and the council doesn't have to worry about employment justice, superannuation, insurance and what have you. Efficiency. But that word, 'efficiency' concealed a great deal of old-fashioned shafting. Anyway, Les and seven others were dumped from the council. But over at Open Family, Father Bob was asking how his mob could get Twentyman's services. And he was told: "Just ask him". Which he did. And I said: "You bet." After two weeks of unemployment, I was back on board.

Bob didn't know it, but a coup was about to unfold at Open Family. The new CEO there, Sue Renkin, had plans for the organisation that didn't include its founder. Sue was one of a generation of people who'd gone into community service with her head full of ideas to make outreach more accountable. Some of her ideas were good, some a bit callous. The vision was to give community service the same priorities as those that governed the running of a private company. This meant mission statements and 'outcomes' that could be shown to represent value for money. Now, I have to admit that there's nothing wrong with a community service mob being made to run properly, decent accountability and all that. But you don't want to give up what you believed in back at the beginning. Bob started Open Family to address the crying need for intervention in the lives of people who were out there on the margins, often completely fucked up. He didn't have a 'mission statement'. He didn't have a list of 'outcomes'. He wanted to put his head and his heart to good use, to see if he could make a difference. And sure, you can introduce a few 'efficiencies' into the place, buy home-brand tea at the supermarket for the office tea caddy, home-brand sugar, all of that sort of thing, but bugger me, remember that your best resource is your heart—that's where it all starts. Once the corporate-minded CEOs take over, there's not so much heart. The CEOs' thinking goes like this: "Heart? Well, goodness me. Can 'heart' give you an outcome?"

Over to Open Family goes Les, and it's all hunky dory at first. I'm doing what I've always done, down there: battling away to get kids back to school and to spare other kids any experience of the Criminal Justice System. Then the suits move against Bob—the male suits, the female suits. They want to get rid of him. The thing with Bob is that he's out of fashion, so the suits opine. Old school, more heart than head—he's gotta go. I've been harping away at this, but let me say again that the suits wanted Open Family to achieve the status of a business, while Bob wanted something with soul. He's a terrific soul, Bob, although I think in his racket you're not supposed to talk about good souls and rubbish souls, just souls. Anyway, Bob's suddenly not there—here yesterday, gone today. Another thing that upset the suits was Bob's sense of humour, his satire, his irony. If there's one thing more than another that distresses the suits, it's a sense of humour. I wonder if you've noticed that humourless people are dangerous types. A sense of humour goes hand-in-hand with a recognition that life on our planet is vast and crazy and magnificent, and very bloody complicated. Without a sense of humour, people are likely to come to dumb, fucked-up decisions because they don't see that huge canvas of life.

And, Jesus! Didn't Bob need a sense of humour; at the very least, to survive the childhood he was dished out. Alcoholic father who went the wallop on Bob using a belt, fists, anything that could be wielded without leading to a homicide conviction. You have a dad like Bob's, you're going to have to find some generosity in your heart to save yourself from toxic loathing. Bob, as a kid, dragged the wretched fellow home from the gutter often enough. That's generosity. My own childhood in comparison, was a stroll in the park with lemonade served in silver goblets. It was his mum Bob relied on as an example of forbearance and fortitude. Beaten bloody, she maintained a grace that Bob admired. He had to find some of that grace himself when, as I say, people with about one-tenth of his character and courage showed him the door at Open Family. Father Bob didn't deserve that. Which only goes to show that you don't have to be dead to be stiff. He's got something to replace Open Family now—the Father Bob Maguire Foundation. Does the same sort of things as Open Family, but with more heart.

Bob's great hero is Jesus, and good on him for that. Jesus wasn't the sort of bloke you could shout a pot of the amber fluid, more the sort who sits over a single glass of shiraz for a couple of hours. He would have been happiest wandering about the outdoors in his kaftan, Jesus, scaling hills to spruik for love and charity, stopping by the temple to upturn tables and deliver a tongue-lashing to the scam artists of Jerusalem. What Bob finds to admire in Jesus, as I suspect, is not his lineage, directly descended from God Almighty and so on, but his more human qualities—courage, conviction, especially his generosity toward sinners. I think he sees Jesus as one of those people who keep the world turning on its axis; who makes a future for the human race possible. And as a matter of fact, that's exactly the way I think of Bob. He makes it possible to imagine a future.

14

The Grim Reaper

Do you know that song, 'Into each life some rain must fall ...'? I've had to cope with a couple of cloudbursts in my time, same as everyone else. And like everyone else, I gave myself up to self-pity, but only for about five minutes. I don't go on with it for long. A little bit of, 'Poor Les! What did I ever do to deserve this?' and another voice in my head says: "Bloody hell, Les. What does anyone do to deserve anything? Shut up." If you keep going down that road of self-pity, very soon you begin to think of yourself as a victim; to define yourself as a bloke picked out from millions for special suffering.

It's 2006, and I'm out walking the dogs in Footscray—Ordinary and Banjo, a couple of boxers—early one morning. There's a wet patch on the footpath, Banjo gives a big yank on his leash and I go down like a hundred-weight sack of spuds falling off the back of a truck. I thought: "Les, you've done some mischief to your leg, you old fool". Bloody agony. The place I'd chosen for this catastrophe was a little out of the way. I can't move, so nothing to do but lie there in my misery with the stupid dogs licking my face. Eventually a big Islander bloke happens along and notices me there off the footpath. "Hey bro," he said, "looks like you might need a bit of help." We arrange an ambulance and I'm into the hospital for operations and whatnot, followed by lengthy rehab. I'd torn the ligament away from the bone in my right leg. Nasty business. These times when you're suffering injury and working your way through recovery, you find yourself with more leisure than you can enjoy—you know, sitting around. And as you're sitting there, you gaze about left and right in your living room and concede that the telly is showing its age and the carpets are looking a bit threadbare; and throughout the house, everything you own is a little on the worn side.

When this happened to me—the enforced leisure thing—I allowed myself to fantasise about the life I might have led. And I'm thinking I wouldn't mind experiencing wealth for a week or so, just to see what it's like. I've never a cared about money, never even see the utility bills—they're all taken care of by the accountant. You see something you like in the shops and think: "I'll have that". Fancy a holiday, get your PA to book the seats business class to Italy, to Portofino—no what am I saying? Business class, be damned—first class! Or New York City, it could be. Nice suite at the Plaza up there on Fifth Avenue. Bloody oath. I've enjoyed a good life, rich with experience, the best friends in the world, the opportunity to reach out to people who desperately needed a helping hand. It's been a first-class life—not business, certainly not economy—a genuine first-class life, when it comes to substance. And the ligament grew itself back to the bone. I lived to walk the stupid dogs again.

Then came the downpour in 2009—no, I didn't see that coming. (It's an extended metaphor, reader—keep up!) I'd had it pointed out to me that I no longer exhibited the slim, boyish build I was once known for. Well, when I say, "once known for" I mean back in the days of Bob Menzies; back in the days of the HR Holden and the first Ford Falcon. A long, long ago. I had a mate, Ron Page, who was no stranger to the chocolate éclair with his cup of coffee, also a bosom buddy of the Big Mac with chips. You couldn't get a metre tape measure around his middle. Ron took himself off to hospital for a lap-band op. You know the lap-band op? They open you up with a machete, grab hold of your stomach, put a rope around it, then draw it tight. It does away with half your appetite. You can only get part way through your Big Mac before you start to feel full. Ron says: "Look into it, Les. Best thing a fat bloke can do for himself."

Call me vain, but I hadn't given up the idea of earning a subsidiary income as a male model. I accepted Ron's advice, took myself off to the Alfred Hospital at the appointed time, the surgeon put the machete to work, lassoed my stomach and stitched me up with sailmaker's yarn. So far, so good. But not long after the op my innards went berserk, I fell into a coma, doctors and nurses running hither and yon (so I was told) shouting, "Les Twentyman's falling to bits! Gotta save Les! All hands on deck!" Exhaustive exploration of the Twentyman system revealed that I had a temperature like that on the surface of the sun and a series of ruptures, or hernias, that threatened to finish me off. They gave me state-of-the-art antibiotics, then got to work again with the machete and stitched up the hernias. Wheeled me back into the recovery ward. But my prospects looked poor. My wife, Cherie, was at my bedside, and the surgeon told her that I probably wouldn't see another sunrise. Amongst my visitors was the Angel of Death hovering impatiently above my bed. I remember distinctly what he said: "All over, Red Rover". And I remember, distinctly, what I replied: "Fuck off". Various people with a reasonably high opinion of me were informed, and the media people began to edit my epitaph. "Sad days, well-known troublemaker and stirrer from the west, Les Twentyman, who devoted a big part of his life to disadvantaged kids has shuffled off the mortal coil, fallen off the perch, turned up his toes. Will be missed." But what do you think? Les revived. Yes, this book is not me speaking from beyond the grave, it's me speaking in the here and now. The doctors put me into an induced coma to give the poor old patched up Twentyman body a better chance to cope with the golden staph that was making a nuisance of itself in my system.

A strange thing, but while I was in this coma, more pipes feeding into me and out of me than tunnels in the Snowy scheme, I enjoyed, off and on, a type of blurry awareness of what was going on. I could hear Cherie's voice murmuring comforting things; sometimes Jenny Cope's voice reading to me from a novel. It was a pleasant sensation, as if we were all wandering around in a fog. In this fog, I could occasionally make out dim lights, or auras. But I can't claim any near-death experiences; didn't see Our Heavenly Father, or Jesus up ahead saying: "Les, my boy, come this way, come towards the light".

I was three weeks in this coma before the doctors allowed me to return to the world. Bloody hell, I was bandaged up like an Egyptian mummy. I thought: "Les, what was the point? You came in here without any hernias, no golden staph, and now you've got both. So, what was achieved?" Well, I can say this. Ernest Hemingway wrote that reading epitaphs about yourself was deeply satisfying. It was thought that he'd died in a plane crash in Kenya, and newspapers were full of notices of his passing. Then he walked out of the jungle, still alive, and had the opportunity to read all about his life and career and lamented passing. I had lots of the people I love expressing their affection for Poor Old Les on His Deathbed. So, that's one good thing. Nice to know that people keep you in their hearts.

15
Which Side Are You On?

I don't want anyone to think I'm giving a blast on my own bugle if I say that I know my turnips from my parsnips when it comes to dealing with the media. I wasn't born knowing what was what; I had to learn it. And what I learnt was that the media is us. We get the media we deserve. No use saying that the current affairs people on telly don't give you a fair shake—whoever you are. They give you the shake that plays loudly out in viewerland. I might want a ten-minute spot on News at Nine to give my POV on the Apex boys, but the producer says: "Can give you maybe 45 seconds, Les, unless you've got something new—Apex boys getting ready to detonate a thermonuclear device, something like that?" If I'm on the *7.30 Report* on the ABC, sure, I might get the attention of Leigh Sales for ten minutes. And every now and again they might give me a couple of minutes on *A Current Affair*, or *Today Tonight*.

The biggest audience is the tabloid audience, and without that thermonuclear device, they're going to say: "Les, forty-five seconds, make your point". The tabloid folk on commercial telly, in the newspapers, or the radio, they know what they're working with. Viewers, listeners, readers, they want three things: outrage, tears, heroics. A story about a dog that jumps off St. Kilda Pier and saves a drowning toddler—brilliant. Or the dog saves the toddler, but the pooch drowns in the process—tears, but brilliant. Or both the dog and the toddler are left to struggle while an unemployed youth with a cannabis habit watches on, too stoned to do anything—outrage, also brilliant.

The tabloid folk, they're avid for stories that are in the slot—outrage, tears, heroics—but sometimes they need to give the story a tweak. So, let's say that a government minister goes to the pulpit to say something disparaging about the unemployed. See, unemployment is high, about 10%, and the government is worried that the electorate might think it's the government's fault. No, no, says the minister, it's the fault of the unemployed. Kids who don't want to work, who prefer sit-down money whilst they lounge around drinking beer, smoking cigarettes and eating takeaway from KFC. And *A Current Affair* gives the minister a couple of minutes to make his case. Bit of a response from viewerland, and the producer thinks: "Hmm, might tweak this, spill a bit of blood on the sawdust". He needs to make it more of a human drama; he sends a reporter out to find some of these lazy unemployed kids who sit on their arses and won't work. And the reporter finds the Paxtons.

I knew the Paxtons before they became famously vilified all over Australia. The family lived out in the west, in working-class St. Albans. I'd come to know the mum of the family, Dawn, fine woman, big heart, would sometimes take in a homeless kid and give him or her a place to sleep and a decent feed. Four kids of her own, and the youngest was Craig. Now, the cops out west, what can I say? Some good 'uns, but some not so good, capable of picking an easy target and bringing down grief. The cops saw young Craig walking home from the shops at 10.30 one night—he was fourteen at the time—and decided they didn't like the cut of his jib. "What're you doing out at this time of night, kid? Up to no good. Did you say something? Did you? Don't say nothin' unless you're asked." That sort of thing—really, just the cops amusing themselves. Dawn got into contact with me, and she was upset. You don't want to see your kid picked on. "Can you do something, Les?" I could. I went to the station and spoke to the cops, nothing heavy, merely pointed out that the kid was okay, didn't deserve the grief. And the two cops listened to what I had to say—to do them what credit I can—and said: "Okay, Les. We'll leave him be, on your say-so."

That was 1995. A year later, a couple of journos at *The Sunday Age* became interested in the 'human face of unemployment' and knocked up some plans to do a study of a whole family on the dole. It was a sympathetic piece, *The Sunday Age* being a centre-left rag. The family they chose was the Paxtons. The journos had probably applied to Centrelink for candidates, and they were given the Paxtons, as fate would have it. Now, the Paxton family comprised Dawn and her four kids—Shane, Mark, Bindi and Craig. Craig, as I mentioned, was the youngest, fifteen in 1996; Bindi came next, at sixteen, then Shane at eighteen and Mark at nineteen. The old man wasn't around. Craig was still in high school; Mark, Shane and Bindi had left school and were on the dole. The three of them had looked for work, but hadn't found anything they could give themselves to, anything that engaged them. This didn't mean that they'd never been offered jobs, just that the jobs they'd been offered were a bit putrid. All three were willing to work, but not at any old job in the world. That's okay. The kids weren't asking for luxury, merely something a bit more engaging than part-time on the counter at a fish and chip shop.

The people at *A Current Affair* in Sydney—Mike Munro particularly, a flinty-hearted son-of-a-bitch if ever there was one—also became attracted to offering their viewers a story about people on the dole. But they were thinking of an outrage yarn, not the sympathetic tale told by *The Sunday Age* folk. The people at *A Current Affair* were canny. Of all the 'hook' stories that journalists adore, the outrage story is the most potent. The hero story is wonderful, but only good for a day or two. After that, viewers become bored. Okay, a bloke jumped off St. Kilda pier and rescued a grandma with a prosthetic leg, well and good, we've applauded him, let's move on. Or such-and-such a person gave his liver, both kidneys and his pancreas to save a mate with only a month to live. Buckets of tears, okay, we've honoured him, let's move on. But oh, my goodness, whip up some outrage and it runs from the consciousness of the public like lava from an erupting volcano.

The producer at *ACA* in Sydney, together with presenter, Mike Munro, saw in the Paxtons a source of outrage that would amount to a veritable Vesuvius. They couldn't tell the Paxton kids of their scheme—of course, not. They allowed the kids to believe that this was to be a sympathetic story, like the one in *The Sunday Age*. And now, right here, after the arrival of the camera crew from ACA, is when I want to be with the Paxtons. The kids are up and about when the crew arrives, and the producer asks them to get back in bed. Why? Because they're going to be characterised as lazy little bastards, so they should be in bed at midday. If I'm there, I'd say: "Kids, no way. Stay exactly where you are." By the time I'd finished dispensing my advice to the kids, there wouldn't have been a story, and the *ACA* camera crew and producer and reporter would have packed up and gone back to the studio in despair. But I wasn't there, and the lives of Shane, Bindy and Mark became an adventure playground of moral indignation for *ACA*.

The Paxton saga was rating through the roof on *ACA*. The *ACA* audience itself is broadly tabloid, which is to say, ready at a moment's notice to cross that frontier from simple engagement into hysteria. And they want to see punishment. That's important, the punishment bit. Centrelink was reviewing the kids' dole payments, but that wasn't enough to satisfy the hunger for punishment. The *ACA* people saw the opportunity to take the story to a new level. Mike Munro, a man who never saw a scruple he wasn't willing to ignore, phoned Dawn Paxton with an offer of employment for her kids. The jobs weren't in St. Albans, where the Paxtons lived; they weren't in Melbourne at all, nor even in Victoria. They were up at a holiday resort on South Molle Island, off the Queensland coast. The resources of Channel 9 might have found jobs for the Paxtons three thousand kilometres closer to home, but the resort gave the *ACA* producer fabulous shots of beaches and girls in bikinis and sunny skies. The suggestion was this: "Jobs in paradise. If the Paxton kids won't accept employment in paradise, then everything we know about dole bludgers and the youth of today are true, and we are showing you the worst of living examples?"

Now, leaving home for the first time to travel three thousand kilometres to the coast of Queensland was daunting to the kids. Bindi was in a band and it was a sorrow to her to abandon her mates. Also, her boyfriend, who would remain in Melbourne. But the kids could see the set-up by now—if they said 'No', they would be confirmed out in viewerland as the vilest sort of dole bludgers. So they reluctantly agreed to go to South Molle Island and take up the jobs. *ACA* was in a win-win situation. Kids won't hack it—big viewer outrage response; kids stay—big viewer response to the concern and generosity of the *ACA* people.

Well, the kids didn't stay. They hated the resort. The jobs were shit, not what they'd been told to expect. All the same, the kids didn't object; they rolled up their sleeves and toiled away. But the resort management people treated them as if they were a lower life form from another planet; snide, disparaging comments. They wanted Bindy to wear a uniform that she took one look at and dismissed, and they wanted Shane and Mark to have their long hair cut in a sort of South Molle nice-boy style. The boys said no. They were lonely, the kids, but more than anything else, they'd become aware of just how completely they'd been gamed; turned into fodder for television. If they'd been treated decently, given a friendly welcome, the haircuts and uniforms and shit jobs wouldn't have mattered. They came home to St. Albans, and *ACA* butchered them. Journalists waited outside the Paxton home in cars, waiting for any of the family to poke his or her head out of the door. You know the way it works. A reporter with a mike, a camera crew ready to shoot gets right into the face of the subject with provocative statements disguised as questions. "Bindy, Bindy! How does it feel to be a dole bludger? Dawn, are you happy to be the mother of the laziest kids in Australia?" Oh yeah, it was a rich lode of outrage that Vesuvius was spewing out.

And the witch hunt was on. Big time. Members of the public were ringing up Dawn and the kids and uttering death threats. John Laws, on 2UE in Sydney, did his grotesque moral indignation schtick, speaking of the kids as 'those putrid Paxtons'. Watching on, I was made sick to my stomach, and I thought of times past when crowds attended public executions, crazed with a hunger for death and suffering. Yeah, I wished with all my heart I'd been in the Paxtons' corner at crucial stages in the unfolding drama. Like I said, we get the media we deserve. It's us. I love my fellow man and woman, sure, but quite a few of my fellow human beings have bloody dodgy ideas of justice. If they didn't see things through this red mist of hatred for the people that *ACA* wants to vilify, the show would never have been made. The hate mail that was delivered to the Paxton house—it came in bloody bushel-loads. And there was a program on Triple M that handed out cash and CDs to a couple of girls who claimed they'd met up with Bindy Paxton on the street and bashed her.

The General Manager of Channel Nine in Melbourne, Ian Johnson, was a bit of a mate of mine; both of us deeply involved in the Williamstown Footy Club. We'd sat together at Willy games, sampling the amber fluid, got on well. I called him up to complain about the shoddy way the Paxtons were being treated on *ACA*. Said he couldn't help me, although he was sympathetic. "*ACA*'s out of Sydney," he said. "Don't have any say-so up there." Not long after speaking to Ian Johnson, I was invited to put my oar in at 3AW, the Stan Zameski program, but it all ended in tears. Stan was on one his rants, damning the Paxton kids to hell.

His producer called me back after I'd hung up and wanted me to speak to Stan again. I told him that Stan had the mentality of a Third Reich Jew killer. "He'd send every kid on the dole to the gas chambers if he could." Fair enough, I might concede that I went too far, but fucking hell, not by much. You see what happens if you give vilification free rein? It brings out the disgusting worst in people. When Hitler started out all he had was verbal abuse. He 'wins office', and ten years later the verbal abuse has become mass murder. We've got the institutions in Australia that would save kids on the dole from the gas chambers, but the appetite for murder is there, for sure.

We got some of our own back a little later when I was invited onto *ACA* to chat with Ray Martin. *ACA* was still enjoying its protracted period of rant about the Paxton kids. Ray raised the whole thing about Shane, Mark and Bindy abandoning their jobs at the South Molle Island Resort which gave me the chance to jump in with a story I'd confirmed about a girl who'd worked at the resort without ever getting paid. But my research had gone a bit further than that. I revealed to *ACA* audience that the South Molle resort was not only bankrupt but was in court with the Tax Office for seven million bucks in unpaid taxes. Mike Munro was on screen at the Sydney studios of Channel Nine. I told him that he was bankrupt himself, morally bankrupt, going after the Paxton kids when he was on the bankroll of one of the richest blokes in Australia. Well, fuck me, it was a point that had to be made. If Munro couldn't see how dodgy his situation was, someone had to tell him. Another thing he needed to be told was that the resort manager admitted he'd taken the Paxtons on as a publicity stunt, expecting terrific PR for his shonky enterprise.

We kicked a couple of goals, sure. And John Safran, the comedian, kicked another beauty from the centre square when he collared Ray Martin outside his house and demanded to know why he was home at 10 o'clock in the morning. This was one of the accusations that *ACA* had made about the Paxtons—home in the middle of the morning instead of being out working. Safran asked if Martin considered himself a bludger. And John had Shane with him, grinning his head off. Ray, he wasn't best pleased, it would be fair to say. Love John. Watching him carrying out that stunt, or anything he does, and you have to admire the way he never takes a step back. You need balls for that, you bet.

You know the old union song: 'Which Side Are You On'?

Come all you good union men,
Good news to you, I'll tell
Of how that good old union
Has come in here to dwell.

Which side are you on, boys,
Which side are you on?
Which side are you on, boys,
Which side are you on?'

The Great Big Paxton Saga, that was one of those 'which side are you on' moments. Because you need to know which side you're on, straight away. Are you with the conceited bullies like Alan Jones, John Laws, Stan Zameski and Mike Munro, ready to stick your finger in the eye of kids like Mark and Bindy and Shane, eager to find how much pain you can cause? Or are you on the side of the kids with no power, no media savvy—such easy pickings? Which side are you on? I'd never say that you have to be on the side of the working class just for the sake of it, or that every working-class bloke is a paragon of virtue. Hell no. I've known people from the working class you'd catch a train to a distant location just to avoid. But look at the bigger picture. The conceited bullies, and the easy targets. Do you want to side with John Laws? With Stan Zameski? Do you want to be known as the sort of gutless wonder who would never in a million years dream of taking on a critical story about Kerry Packer (yeah, God rest his soul, I suppose) but can't wait to get at those who don't know what sort of game you're playing? And even if the Paxton kids had been the sort of idle bastards depicted in the media (which they weren't), would that be a profitable employment of your time? Working yourself into a frothing frenzy about three kids on the dole? Which side are you on, boys, which side are you on?

I can tell you a tale about taking a side just to round things off. In 2010, the Dalai Lama made one of his visits to the sunburnt country and asked his organisers (there were a few of them) to arrange to have people in the audience who worked with struggling kids—the very kids in the LTF programs. And as fate would have it, I was recommended to the Dalai Lama's people. They asked my mate, Chris Hooper, to ask me if I'd come along to an audience in Footscray, Maddern Square, where there'd probably be thousands turning up. I said: "What? The Dalai Lama?" Chris said: "Yep, wants you there, mate. You'll do the introductions. Big opinion of you." I said: "The Dalai Lama? You're pulling my leg, aren't you?" And Chris: "No way, my friend. They're sending some folk out to your place to have a chat, give you the protocols." Well, they did send some folk out to vet me, not once but six times. Asked all sorts of questions. The thing is, they didn't want me to suddenly reveal that I had a penchant for torturing small animals with meat skewers, or that I was a bigamist, maybe a drunkard. I think they were just trying to get a read on me and, after all their questions, they seemed content. But one final question: "Mr Twenty, are there any people who consider you an enemy? Bad opinion of you? Might want to shoot you?" I gave a great hoot of laughter. "Anyone thinks I need shooting? Yeah, a few. The queue starts in City Square and ends in Warrnambool."

"Ha, ha, ha! Very good joke, Mr Twenty! Ha, ha, ha!" Who's joking?

Ultimately, I was approved. Six hundred kids from Footscray City High were approved, too. And hosts of other folk, pretty much approved. Up on a raised platform for the sake of being viewed, sat the Dalai Lama, looking composed and sublime. A long queue of well-wishers shuffled along to exchange a few words with the great man. I'd heard that people about to meet the Dalai Lama could sometimes become a bit shaky, even faint dead away. The explanation was that the Dalai Lama radiated this terrifically powerful aura, and if you were a bit susceptible to that sort of thing, might overwhelm you. I was feeling a bit shaky myself before I introduced him, nervous, sort of stage fright. I got through the speech, sure, but resuming my seat immediately afterwards, my daks split up the inside of one thigh. I thought: "Bloody hell!" Because here I was hosting this guy with the holiest vibe of all time and I'm in danger of having the family jewels fall out of my daks. Cherie, seated close by, was gesturing furiously to me and mouthing the words: "Your trousers!" What the hell could I do? I managed as best I could to avoid embarrassment, and was alert enough to hear the Dalai Lama whisper into my ear—I was seated beside him—"I want to make a donation to your charity of one hundred dollars". And I was like: "Yeah, sweet, thanks for that". Then one of his people whispered something to him, and the Dalai Lama gestures for me to lean closer. "I mean one hundred thousand dollars." I was flabbergasted. But I managed to give the holy bloke a huge smile of appreciation. So, you see what I'm getting at? The Dalai Lama chose a side. And it was our side, he chose. The side of the angels.

A brief postscript to this tale of the visitor from Tibet. I was asked to introduce him a second time, in 2013, this time at Geoff's Shed—otherwise known as the Convention Centre—in front of a crowd of six thousand. I said gidday, gave a little bow. I said: "Thanks so much for that hundred thousand, Your Holiness. Made a big difference to our mob." And what did the Dalai Lama say: "Oh, you remember that?" Now that's genuine humility. So, good to have him on our side.

Magda Szubanski was the MC and was great. I still got stage fright—the larrikin from Footscray in the presence of this famous leader for good in the world. Later, as soon as I could, I hightailed it out the back to a pub over the road for a pick-me-up. Next thing Magda and her mates came in—they seemed to feel like me—awed and honoured and privileged to have played a part at this memorable occasion, and needing a drink.

16

This Life

This is one of those days when I break out the Giorgio Armani (note to my stalker: only joking, dummy) apply some black Kiwi to the Florsheims, sort through my Henry Bucks' Slim Line shirts, and drag the hairbrush through my flowing locks. It's Launch Day. The Twentieth Man is about to become The Les Twentyman Foundation, streamlined for the twenty-first century. A lot of brain work has gone into the transition; David Young, the chairman of the foundation, a big contributor of time and IQ, and Wayne Owen. We're in the dining room of the pavilion at the Trevor Barker Oval in Sandringham, home of the marauding Zebras, two hundred and thirty people, most of them supporters of The Twentieth Man, and now of the

Foundation. Captains of industry so thick on the carpet here that if a comet hit the pavilion, the stock exchange would have to close for six months. And sporting legends, including Leigh (Lethal) Matthews looking dapper, considered by those who would know to be the greatest Aussie Rules player ever to have pulled on a guensey. Leigh has agreed to act as an ambassador for the Foundation, and I couldn't be more grateful. He's surrounded by people asking him questions about his life in footy: "Leigh, the 1983 Grand Final—toughest game Hawthorn ever played?" "Leigh, about Huddo, was he the best full forward ever?" "Leigh, the Hawks three premierships as good at the Lions?"

He's good-natured, Lethal, answers every question with a smile. The reason I wanted him as an ambassador for the Foundation is that he has credibility out in the community. And he's articulate, unusual in a sportsman. Publicity is important. You know how many charities there are in Australia? More than a hundred thousand, new ones hoisting their banner every week. You have to shine, or you're lost. It was a lesson I took to heart early on, making yourself known. I thought: "Les, speak up, tell people what you're doing and why you're doing it". I'm considered a genuine loudmouth in certain quarters, won't shut up, can't be shut up, but if I'm drawing attention to myself it's not for my own glorification. It's for the poor mugs no one will listen to.

I'm on a table in front with nine guests. Kelvin Thompson's across from me; getting out of politics after about five hundred years, Kelvin is. He's been good to us. He was Parliamentary Secretary under Kevin 07, and under Julia; shadow minister when Labor was out of government. Bernie Finn's here, member for Western Met in the Legislative Council, decent sort of supporter of ours; also, Pat Boyle from the wallopers who's been a terrific help down the years; used to be in charge of the Asian Squad at Vic Pol, more of a Gentleman Copper these days; written a learned thesis on crime and policing. Pat's an example of the sort of copper who sees all the limitations of policing in the rough and tumble west. I used to contact Pat when I needed to get something straight about one client or other, maybe a bloke claiming he's an innocent party in some world-wide conspiracy of bad guys. Pat would say: "Not such an innocent party, Les. Kitted out with a grenade launcher and an AK when we picked him up." Okay, not quite as severe as that, but something like it. He tells a story of a young girl up in front of the judge who's likely to be returned to the care of her mum, except her mum's mostly out of her brain on all sorts of gear. Pat sees disaster looming, but there's nothing he can do, nothing much the judge can do, either. Legislation can never cover every contingency. If Pat wants to keep the kid out of the care of her arsehole of a mother, he needs something in writing that proves the mother is incompetent. And the judge would need to see it, too. But there's no document available from the DHS to say that the mum is mad on gear. Heartbreaking for Pat, tough on the beak. Catalogues of sad stories like that in policing. And something not recognised in the general public is that most coppers care about this sort of thing. They hate to see a kid put back in harm's way.

I'm sitting here looking out at the bay that's as calm as a duck pond, grey sky hanging low over the water, not a breath of wind. All around me, cheerful people who pat me on the back and murmur: "Well done, Les. Great day, Les." Well, yeah, it's a big day, but the thought keeps nagging at me that right now, something's going down out there in the west that'll need attention in the next twenty-four hour: some kid chased out of his home by a ratbag father, getting ready to doss down under a hedge in a park, a pile of newspaper for a pillow. What makes me proud, what makes me glad, is not so much a fancy sit-down lunch for two-hundred and thirty people and slaps on the back; no, it's the times when we get to that kid before he accepts that dealing is his only path to a square meal; get to him, find him a place to kip, nudge him back to school. Just that.

We've got Gary Sweet along as the MC—huge on the telly for decades, Gary, and a contributor to The Twentieth Man for a while now. I look fabulous in my million-dollar threads, but you should take a gander at Gary. Trim and handsome in his duds, and his Florsheims really *are* Florsheims. The ladies in the audience will need to be restrained before long, squirming about on their seats and getting ready to charge the stage. Gary has some nice things to say about me, also a lot of amusing things to say about himself. You wouldn't know listening to him that his commitment to the cause is as sincere as it is. He's not about to brag.

The waiters serve the tucker, choice of crumbed chicken or roast beef with gravy and veg, swap them about if you don't get what you want. Lots of lovely wine. The guests hoe in as David Young, Chairman of the Foundation, waxes lyrical about our achievements over the years. Another handsome chap, David; our board is full of good looking blokes, lady killers. Just worked out that way. He's an orthopaedic surgeon, a list of credentials as long as your arm, none more impressive than his role as orthopaedic surgeon to the Western Bulldogs. He'll be hard at work on Bob Murphy's ACL after Sunday's game against Hawthorn. Consultant orthopaedic surgeon to the Australian and Victorian Sports Institutes, and Netball Australia. Also, a member of the Australian Knee Society. What in God's name is that? Anyway, a bloke full of the good stuff. Something you notice in my line of work is how many professionally successful people find the time to help out. It's one of the reasons I've never been a barrow pusher for any political party. I've heard Labor Party people banging on about the wealthy and their wickedness, and yeah, there's a few wicked 'uns out there, but just as many or more of the successful are on the side of the angels, who roll up their sleeves and get into fundraising. David isn't wealthy, but he's not short of a quid, esteemed in his profession. With all that's on his plate, you wouldn't think he could find two minutes in a row to give to his work at the Foundation. But he finds plenty of time—plenty. You want something done, give the job to a busy man. Or a busy woman. We've got our share of the fair sex pitching in.

You know what makes the difference between those who help out and those who don't? It's this. The helpful grasp how a community works. They know that it's a complex thing, a great big community. They know that social legislation is designed to give some support for those who are battling to make sense of their lives in the community; make a go of it. But there are hundreds of ways in which people struggle to make it happen in that great big society, and legislation doesn't cover everything. Nobody starts out life thinking: "Smack—gotta get me some of that". They get sucked in; things are going poorly in one way and another and they want some instant gratification. And nobody thinks: "A life of crime and wholesale violence, yeah, get me started". It's just that swinging a fist or sticking a gun in somebody's face is the limit of their imagination. You've got to do more than simply chase down the addicts and the people who rely on violence to solve their problems. You've got to find ways to intervene before things go rotten. And in a society like ours, we're asking those with the wherewithal to make a commitment to those who don't have it. Without the private commitment of the David Youngs, we're stuffed. They make what we've got, possible; a community that hangs together, just about. End of the Les Twentyman sermon on social cohesion. But don't worry—there's plenty more to come.

That glassy bay out there. I'm thinking: "That's what I want, one day. The whole of the west like a smooth sea, no wind, no waves, peace and quiet." Yeah, well it's not going to happen, is it? Still, a bloke can dream.

Wayne Owen's up on the stage. Wayne's our CEO, fabulous organiser, fabulous administrator. He's letting everyone know that he's the sort of bloke who won't see a cent of the Foundation's budget wasted. He's a complete budget zealot, Wayne is. Give him a dollar, he wants 99.5 cents of that to go into the programs. The place has to run on the remaining 0.5 of a cent. Need a pencil sharpener for the office? No way. Use a kitchen knife. Want a cuppa? Use every teabag twice. He's had an audit of budget effectiveness done by a bunch of hard nuts, and it turns out the Fund gets $11.50 of value out of every dollar spent on the programs. The man's a genius.

I get my chance to say something. Bloody hell, the public speaking I've done over the years. Thousands of times, no fear of exaggeration. You know where it started, me trying to inspire an audience with my silver tongue? Down at the footy ground when I was in Year 10 at Braybrook High School. We were playing Altona High School, 'traditional rivals' as they say. Those boys at Altona were tough little buggers, but so were we. Wore barbed wire singlets and breakfasted on brick fragments. Anyway, it happens I'm not playing this day; I'd done something to my knee and I'm on crutches. But I'm the captain of the team, so I'm there giving moral support. Three quarter time and we're behind. The coach, Bill Glasson, decent sort of fella and a bloody good teacher, calls me over. "Les, I want you to say something to our kids. Get 'em going. I can't use the words they need to hear, being a teacher. But you can." I gather our boys around and give them the benefit of my wisdom. My wisdom in those days was based on my mastery of four-letter words. "I'm fucking ashamed of the fucking lot of youse, fucking weak as fucking water fucking man-up on the fucking back line I don't fucking want to see that fucking mongrel they've got at fucking full forward touch the fucking ball for the fucking rest of the fucking game." Words to that effect. And I've continued on to the present day, with fewer effings.

I promised you more Twentyman sermons, but I've changed my mind. One day I'll publish all my sermons and outbursts and raves and rants, ten volumes of fine print. So, that's something for you to look forward to. Up on stage, I thank a lot of people from the bottom of my heart, tell a few scurrilous jokes about Dougie Hawkins and a couple about myself. I look out over the assembled multitudes, mike in my hand. It's a good feeling. All of this, the rebranded Fund, it came out of an ache deep in my guts years and years ago at the sight of kids running amok in the streets of Braybrook, dodging school, going absolutely nowhere. I'm a cheerful bloke most hours of the day; brought up by parents who cared about their kids; I had a decent start in life. But back then, seeing those kids on the highway to hell,

I knew I couldn't block them out of my thoughts and just go about making myself happier still. Some people can do that; I can't. You've heard of a cove from the olden days by the name of John Donne, a poet, a real tearaway as a young bloke back in London, chasing sheilas up and down the cobbled streets? Know him? Also, a bit of a scholar when he wasn't dashing off sonnets or shedding his trousers. Somebody mentioned him to me, a writer I know. After a while, John Donne gives himself to religion, feels he has to make a commitment to his fellow man. He wrote a poem that begins, "No man is an island," and after a certain amount of too-ing and fro-ing reaches the conclusion that none of us can exist just for ourselves. You have to roll up your sleeves and pitch in. "For I am involved in mankind," he says. You hear the church bell ringing and you think: "Okay, that's the funeral knell, who's died?" Donne, he finishes up by saying that it doesn't matter who's died, it's as if the bell is for you, because you and everyone else, you're all joined together in one big community. It's how I feel, maybe in a less fancy way. This is the only life I could have led with a clear conscience.

17

Adventures in Public Speaking

These days I do more public speaking than ever—you can't shut me up—but I've done a fair bit of it ever since the '70s when I first took up youth work. Service clubs, parliamentary groups of one sort and another, coterie gatherings, teachers, preachers, civic groups—I've shown my gorgeous face to all of them, and regaled them with tales from the mean streets. Here's the thing: people want to know what's going on with disadvantaged kids, what's going on in gangland, what's going on in the world of the addict, but they can hardly go wandering up and down the footpaths of Caroline Springs and Braybrook and Sunshine asking those they meet if they're living in blinding poverty or hooked on methamphetamines. They have to rely on me and people like me for news from the frontlines. And yeah, of course I want to tell them, because the people I talk to from the lectern hope to help, if they can. There are literally hundreds of charities or civic organisations that donate to youth work every year, scores that contribute to The Les Twentyman Foundation, and before that, The Twentieth Man. The invitations to talk are more numerous than I can accept, but I try to do my best.

I've had to teach myself how to address an audience, but I have to admit that I started with a big advantage. I was born talking, came into the world with a full vocabulary and a broad set of opinions on damn near everything. At school, I drove the teachers nuts, which is the explanation for my Corridor Education: "Twentyman, get yourself out into the corridor, I'm sick of the sound of your voice." "But, sir, what am I supposed to do in the corridor? I've been out there ten times this week already." I can't be sure, but I think I kept up the chatter even when I was alone. And out on the footy field, oh boy, from the first bounce of the ball until the final siren I'd offer my opinion from close range on the parentage, mental capacity and sexual inadequacy of my opponents. A knack for slinging insults is not the same thing as talking to an audience on any sort of serious issue, though.

I've had to learn to speak in a way that keeps the listeners listening; to tell a story, provide moments of drama and insight. And to avoid the Fidels. You know what happens when you're overcome at the lectern by a severe bout of the Fidels? You do what Castro did, and go on and on and on until the audience wants to drink hemlock. Fidel's audience members at one of his big four-hour speeches, they'd be *forced* to drink hemlock if they yawned or dozed off, and I imagine many of them thought death would be a welcome release. People can only listen for so long before numbness sets in. Fifteen minutes of alert listening is about the average. So I tell myself: "Les, do not bang on". Also: "Les, don't shout". If you get shouty up there on the stage, all you do is alarm people. Sure, show your passion, but not by yelling. I had to learn, too, to make my point. There were times I'd be warbling away up there on the stage, fifty or a hundred or five hundred people listening, all waiting for me to make my point. Because that's what folks are there for—to hear you make your point. If I go gaga with figures and statistics, I have to pull back and remember that all these numbers are supposed to support the need for more investment in accommodation for the homeless, or early intervention programs. If I don't make my point, I notice that puzzled looks break out in the audience.

But even if I pay attention to everything I've learnt as a public speaker, I can still end up pissing somebody off. I was talking to an audience down in Drouin a while ago, a community group, and it behoved me (like that? 'behoved me'—classy, isn't it?) to mention my experiences in Belfast and Northern Ireland generally. The context was my study of the Youth at Risk programs in Northern Ireland.

I happened to speak about meeting Brian Keenan and his IRA comrades, and at the conclusion of my speech a bloke came storming up to me with a face the colour of a beetroot. "I didn't come here to listen to you congratulating the IRA, that gang of murderers and crooks." He had some connection to the Loyal Orange Lodge in Northern Ireland, and seemed to feel that the IRA shouldn't be mentioned anywhere without adding: "Killers and scoundrels". I hadn't been glamourising the IRA—I'd mentioned their extra-judicial punishments, kneecaps, ankles, elbows, the six-pack—but that wasn't enough for this individual. I've come to appreciate the need to hold my tongue when dealing with nutcases. What I really wanted to say was: "Fuck off and stay fucked off." But I keep it courteous. "Hmm, you don't say, well I'm sorry if I've offended you or any of your family or clan or even your remote acquaintances going back ten generations."

The sensitivities of a few people in a big audience, I have to ask myself to what extent I should avoid rousing them up. And then I realised that too much avoidance is going to make a eunuch of me, and I dismissed it. Of course, there are times when I concede that my entire point is to insult a particular person, such as Bruce Ruxton, one time President of the RSL, who was slagging off immigrants and Aboriginal people at a certain stage of his career. I was invited to speak on a radio program about Bruce's grotesque rants, and I took the opportunity to label him a 'geriatric Rambo'. Bruce, much more sensitive to insults directed at him than to those he issued himself, professed himself to be hurt beyond healing by the Twentyman turn of phrase. As were many of his comrades. Radio stations, telly stations, they were avid for more. Viewers and listeners get madly excited by public slanging matches. I obliged with one or two further phrases, but then I dropped it. I didn't want to become known all over the country for an argument with silly old Bruce. Remember I was saying that as a public speaker, you must make your point? Well, all the points I wanted to make were about kids at risk and what could be done.

Then there was the Dougie fracas. By 'Dougie' I mean, of course, the Dougie of Dougies, Dougie Hawkins, legendary wingman for the Scraggers, and a genuine scallywag in all places and at all times. Also, a man with a big heart. Always ready to help out in our programs at The Twentieth Man and lend his name to the lists of celebrated folk willing to stand up for the marginalised. It happens frequently that Dougie and I will find ourselves talking at various functions, not always connected with The Twentieth Man, and it was at one of these affairs that I heard Dougie's immortal 'parachute' yarn. It goes like this: back in the days when Terry Wheeler was coaching the Mighty Scraggers with such panache—the 1990s—he dreamt up a publicity stunt before a final that called for the members of his team to parachute one at a time from the skies above Williamstown down onto Willy Beach. All sorts of media were gathered on the beach to record and praise this noble stunt. So far, so good. Dougie was in the aircraft, waiting to jump. Not so keen, actually, as he imagined himself spread out like a pancake on the beach before the assembled multitudes. The people who were overseeing the jump included a strapping individual whose job it was to say to each of the Scraggers: "Ready … Steady … Jump!" Dougie was the last remaining Scragger to jump, and he remained powerfully reluctant. Dougie said: "I don't wanna do it!" And this strapping fellow looked Dougie straight in the eye and said: "Listen, mister, I've got a Johnson in my trousers a foot long, and if you don't jump, I'm going to shove it straight up your arse". And Dougie, telling the story, says: "So I had to go ahead, didn't I? I'm often asked what it was like. Well, it hurt the first couple of times, but then I got used to it."

It's a yarn designed for sports' nights, and Dougie's had it on high rotation for a while now, and not only with audiences full of blokes primed to laugh like a drain at the tale. There were women in the audience many a time. Never any strife. But this recent occasion when I was addressing an audience, Dougie was out there with the punters doing great justice to the jug of draught on the table. I somehow or other created an opportunity to tell Dougie's story, calling out to him every so often to check the facts. At the conclusion, there were gales of laughter, but further down the track, a letter of indignation arrived signed by a couple of ladies in the audience. Crude, they said. Inappropriate. Insensitive. And yeah, they were right. I apologised to them, of course, I did. I thought: "Leslie, stick to the script for the love of

God". On occasion, I give myself over to entertainment. Can't be helped. I might have been treading the boards of Her Majesty's if things had gone differently.

What about Bendigo? Strife there. Gave a talk at the Chinese Museum on youth issues, unemployment, and what it does to kids to feel themselves unwanted in the workforce. And I happened to say something about the old days when I was a young bloke and so many kids went from school into government jobs, the railways, the tramways, the MMBW (Melbourne Metropolitan Board of Works), State Electricity, into a dozen or more big concerns that have all been privatised since. A bloke in the audience strode up to me after I'd finished and wanted to know by what authority I was encouraging the government to employ more young people. He was dead-set Thatcher is God, against governments owning concerns that should be in private hands, and thought he'd died and gone to heaven when John Howard declared himself a great admirer of Maggie the Magnificent. I listened, raised my eyebrows a few times, may have smiled in an indulgent way. But you can see what I'm getting at. Public speaking on political issues is likely to result in a punch on the nose from aggrieved individuals in your audience. I've said things to audiences that you'd think would get universal agreement: keeping ice out of the reach of kids; weapons out of their hands; hustling them along to the school gate; and seeing that they get at least one square meal in their stomachs each day. But there's always someone who wants to declare outrage. I honestly believe I could give a talk condemning Herod's slaughter of the first-born, only to have someone in the audience march up to me in high dudgeon to say that as monarch, Herod had every right to put children to the sword. No, it's a caper that calls for stamina and endless patience.

But it's worth it. I hardly ever say "No" to anyone who wants me if the subject is youth issues. Because I know damned well how quickly the attention of the public on the plight of struggling kids, of alienated kids can evaporate. People have a lot on their minds. I'm competing with leadership changes in federal politics; with concerns about super and the stock market; with the price of petrol; with grotesque things unfolding on Nauru and Manus; with mass murder in Syria; with droughts and floods and bushfires; with the family budget, and where the money's coming from to get braces on little Janie's teeth. I've worked like a bastard to focus the public's attention on youth issues, and I can't let it slip. I'm on a treadmill, sure, but I have to say, the Twentyman frame and the Twentyman vocal chords are standing up to it. Won't shut up. Can't shut up. Get used to it.

18

Political Animal

Nobody will be surprised to hear that the Twentyman household out in working-class Braybrook was Labor from the front doorstep to the top brick on the chimney. We kids were raised in the folklore of the workers' party. The Foundation Tree, the Shearers' Strike, the Eight-Hour Day, Universal Franchise, the right to withhold your labour, and all those good old ballads of struggle, like the one I've already quoted: 'Which side are you on, boys', 'The Ballad of Joe Hill', even the 'Internationale' and 'The Red Flag'. Yep, I've roared out 'The Red Flag' at rallies or in the bar, a glass of beer clasped in my hand.

LES TWENTYMAN

The workers' flag is deepest red,
It shrouded oft our martyred dead,
And ere their limbs grew stiff and cold,
Their hearts' blood dyed its every fold.

And the chorus, sung as loud as you could:

Then raise the scarlet banner high,
Within its shade we'll live and die!
Though cowards flinch and traitors sneer,
We'll keep the red flag flying here!

In all of my young years in Braybrook, I only ever knew one family who voted Liberal, and I considered that family an oddity, as strange as if all the members of the family had got things so mixed up that they insisted on wearing their pyjamas in the daytime. And when I went to work for the railways, I was elected as union rep, and was damned proud of it. I'm glad of it; glad I was raised in a household that honoured the workers. I mean bloody hell, what sort of traditions do you honour if you're a Liberal? The Great Tradition of Employing Scabs? The Great Tradition of Paying Starvation Wages? And what songs do you sing as a Liberal? Can you think of one? No, boys, no, there isn't one. I was soaked to the bone in stories of struggle, and it made me proud to know which side I was on. But in my adult years, my mature years, when I first learned to distinguish the smell of bullshit blindfolded, I made an enlightening discovery, and it was this: not all the best players are on the one team. Which is to say that you'll find as many rogues on the left as you will on the right. And as many saints.

This discovery of mine was reinforced back in 1992, when I first ran as an independent in the state election of that year. I never would've conceived of such an idea as running against the ALP except that the party bosses had pissed me off by parachuting Jean McLean into the Upper House seat of Western Suburbs for that election. Now, Jean, admirable lady that she was, had no credibility as a candidate out West because she came from a posh suburb very remote from Sunshine, Braybrook, and all the other western struggletowns that made up the electorate. In the ALP of old, you had to live in the electorate you wanted to represent and you had to roll up your sleeves and put in the hard yards, for years. Which was only fair. The parachuting ploy really began with Bob Hawke of Sandringham being plonked down in the safe Labor seat of Wills in the north-west of Melbourne back in—what was it? 1980? Yeah, 1980, when the party tossed out the sitting member, Gordon Bryant—or rather 'encouraged him to retire' in something of the way that an interrogator might 'encourage' some bloke to talk by pulling out his fingernails. The closest Jean had ever come to a western suburbs' dweller was when she went to the Victoria Market with her butler. "Approach that chappie, Jeeves, and purchase me a cauliflower." I thought: "Bugger this!" Registered myself as an independent candidate and got down to haranguing the citizenry: "Vote for me. I've lived here all my life, know the place inside out." The Labor bosses saw me as a threat to their gal and got stuck right into me: "That Les Twentyman, lives in a salubrious mansion in toffy Brighton, drinks champagne out of a slipper, feasts on French paté and caviar". I had, in fact, lived in Brighton for a short time, heeding the advice of the coppers, as I've mentioned elsewhere. I had a madman gunning for me, and the wallopers thought that Brighton would be the best place for Les; a safe place. I read the story based on these ALP dirty tricks in the *Herald Sun* and I thought: "You bastards".

What you need going for you with a dirty trick is a sliver of fact—such as the fact that I had lived in Brighton. Once you have that morsel of fact, you can go to town. And if your opponent doesn't have that morsel of fact, other strategies are employed, such as the time-honoured, 'When did you stop beating your wife?' dodge. You know how that works? A reporter might be sent to poison your well by asking you that very question—when did you stop beating your wife? And you answer: "I have never beaten my wife". The headline reads: 'Candidate Denies Wife-beating Charge'. Any denial of anything by a candidate has the effect of rousing suspicion. Why is the candidate denying the accusation? Must be something buried away somewhere. But okay, I'm not claiming that I was a complete babe-in-the-woods politically. I knew there'd be a certain amount of rough and tumble. What did surprise me was the sheer venom of the ALP campaign against me; the hatred I inspired. I mean, for

Christ's sake, my political sympathies were well known—on the left and for the battlers—but Labor went after me as if I were a far-right capitalist thumper advocating slave labour in the salt mines. That was my moment of discovery, right there. Politics is tribal, and if you're not listening to the chief and you want to step outside the circle of the tribe, you're the enemy and the chief will send assassins armed with hatchets to do you in.

I didn't win the seat, but I did well. So well, in fact, that the Labor bosses got the shivers in 1992 when I threatened to run in the Lower House seat of Williamstown—a seat that the ALP considered a lock for the party. The issue was another parachute job by Labor. The bosses wanted to install a barrister from Brighton as the ALP candidate, a woman of some accomplishment but with no experience of the lives people lived in the electorate. See, when the big parties opt for a parachute job, they show disdain for the voters in the seat. It's as if they're saying: "So our candidate has barely seen the town hall of your electorate, and would normally avoid the dump as if the plague was raging in the streets and alleys. But if you elect our carefully groomed candidate, he or she will hold his or her nose and move in, sure, take up residence, become your pal." My politics are personal, intimate, face-to-face. God knows, I've got my flaws as a human being, but taking people for granted ain't one of 'em. I never pack people by the gross, never deny them their humanity. I want people to vote for me because they have it in their hearts to reach out to the kids I reach out to. I want them to say: "Les, we pretty much trust you to do what we would do". The barrister from Brighton might well have a heart of gold, but unless this individual has smelt the sweat of a man or woman who has toiled all day to keep the wolf from the door, then hell, keep away from a working-class electorate.

My threat did the trick. The Labor bosses could see themselves losing Willy with me on the ballot as an independent. They chose a local instead—Steve Bracks. Steve won the seat and in 1999, led the ALP to government. Is it necessary for me to draw attention to this? To point out that I played my bit in giving the ALP it's most successful, most electable premier of all time? All I can say is that it's a shame if Les has to go about saying, "Good on yer, Twentyman!" when really, reader, that's your job. Keep up!

Trying to get yourself elected to parliament is a schlep, yeah, but not without enjoyment. You go about nattering to anyone who will listen to you, up in front of every sort of community group presenting your credentials, and that's what I do all the time, so it comes easy to me. And I like people, I like meeting them, shaking hands, hearing what they want to tell me. I don't smile my bloody head off like the party candidates—they look like advertisements for Colgate prepared by an agency—but I listen to everyone, even to those who are unlikely to make it to the polling booth on election day. This is democracy, and I love it. In every home in the electorate there's at least one voter, and all of them drive to a polling station or trundle along on their two feet, take a how-to-vote card, make marks on a couple of slips of paper next to the person they most favour, slip the marked papers through a slot in a polling box. All the dirty tricks and lies one candidate has employed against another are in the past. One vote per voter, and that voter's name is crossed off the electoral roll.

I'm face-to-face with people while I help them find food and shelter and education, but I want this for them, too—a good, functioning democracy. Because without that, everything's fucked. Corruption sets in, and the institutions you rely on for impartiality fall to bits. This might sound boring, but what I want for a society—something to go with compassion—is stability. I don't want what they relied on in Belfast: blokes with Glock pistols smashing the kneecaps of kids who've transgressed in some way. A fair and just society, starting at the polling station, where Les is handing out how-to-votes and greeting friends, trading jokes. Smell of snags on the barbie, local primary school reaping the bounty of good Australian charred meat. And the cake stall. God bless the cake stall. Any country that comes up with the idea of raising money for the local primary school by selling snags and cakes on election day is doing okay.

Ran again as an independent in the Upper House seat of Western Suburbs. 1996, that was—the Paxton Election. My support for the Paxtons didn't serve to enhance my popularity, if I can put it in that fancy way. Even amongst working-class people, the demonisation of the Paxtons had taken such a hold that I was poison to the punters. You remember back in the 1950s during the height of the Cold War, how communist sympathisers were made to seem like enemies of Australia? That was me, Les Twentyman, enemy of everything decent and good, out to destroy society. People in the electorate who'd known me for years would shake their heads and say: "Have to part ways with you, Les. Can't stomach those Paxton kids." I was out there every day of the campaign, fighting the good fight, but I could see the votes falling away. And I have to tell anyone thinking of running as an independent, make sure you've got all your friends behind you because you'll want the manpower. Forty or fifty polling booths, and you need someone at every gate to hand out your how-to-vote cards. My Uncle Dookie solved the problem of being in two places at one time at his polling booth by locking the gate of the second entrance, forcing everyone to pass by him at his station. The reps of the other parties called out: "What? You can't lock the gate, Dookie!" And Dookie called back: "Can't hear you, mate, sorry".

My vote in that election came in at 15%—much lower than 1992. I was a disappointed man. Sure, we were going to take a hit, but that big a hit? Really? I had a call from an *Age* reporter who consoled me by pointing out that my vote was greater than all of the other independents combined. But when I run in an election I want to win, bloody oath. Objectively, sure, I can see that it's a bloody big task to take a safe seat from one of the major parties. Who's thinking objectively? It's like footy; I could see myself coming from behind with a late surge, an irresistible force, will you look at that Twentyman go, wow!—he's going to do it, unbelievable, he's going to do it! Except that I didn't. Okay, looking back, what would I prefer?—that I stuck up for the Paxton kids, costing myself thousands of votes, or that I lobbed into the Upper House with a late charge? The kids, absolutely. When Les Twentyman fronts the booth at the pearly gates, St. Peter's going to consult the ledger and say: "Big tick here, in my book, for knowing right from wrong, Les. Step in and make yourself at home, my boy." Well, so I hope.

You'd think I'd had enough. You'd think I'd say to myself: "Les, the parliament caper, you've done your bit, give it a rest, brother". But I ran again in 2006 in the western seat of Kororoit. Now, this election was a bit different from the previous two flirtations with glory. It would've been a monster upset if I'd won in 1992 or 1996. It could have happened, but I was like a horse you take in the Cup at 20 to 1. You study the form, you see a glimmer of hope for your neddy, place your bet and watch him loom in the straight only to be run down a hundred metres from the finishing post. But the electorate of Kororoit out there in the west was made for me. In places it was nitty-gritty, something of the flavour of Sunshine and Braybrook, in other places industrial, also broad areas of new, inexpensive estate housing. The Western Highway ran plumb through the middle of Kororoit, with the Western Ring Road on one side and the Melton Highway on the other. Between the highways, the suburbs of Caroline Springs, Burnside Heights, Deer Park, Rockbank. The electorate was in parts quite affluent, but it also had pockets of dire struggle: people working two or three jobs to keep their heads above water, and big concentrations of disaffected kids looking for work they could stomach—meaning, something a bit more rewarding than handing burger boxes and chip packets out the drive-through window at Maccas. Lots of immigrants out in Kororoit, some of them from countries that had been belted from pillar to post by wars and insurrections. These highway electorates, wherever they are in outer-suburbia all over Australia, are pretty much safe Labor seats. A number of the electors are rusted-on Labor supporters who wouldn't change their party even if the ALP ran a big black dog as a candidate. But the rusted-on are still a minority. The majority is inclined to vote Labor, yeah, but can be persuaded to change. But could they be persuaded to change to Les? Well, maybe. This was to be a by-election, not a full state election. The seat had been held by Andre Haermeyer until he retired mid-term, forcing the by-election. Andre had been an honoured man in the electorate with a huge majority when he ran in 2004. The Labor voters adored him. Now that he'd pulled the plug, many of the Kororoit electors would re-assess their vote, so I had that going for me. The Kororoit folk were free to look around and ask what the ALP had done for them after six years in power. And they'd be forced to conclude: not that much.

The Labor candidate was Marlene Kairouz, not so popular with some of the unions that would normally back anyone Labor put up. The Electrical Trades Union secretary, Dean Mighall, spoke to me and said that the ETU would back me, an independent. A big boost for the Twentyman cause! I said: "Ta, Dean, I love you, too". Then a setback. Well, politics is a tactical game with a sort of series of advances and setbacks—you have to cop it sweet. This setback concerned another of the independent candidates, Tania Walters, a pro-life activist. She'd been intending to direct her preferences to me, even though I had a pro-choice record. She invited me to her main rally of the election, big pro-life jamboree, photographs of foetuses in the womb, seriously emotional slogans about mass murder and what have you, comparing the pro-choice people to Eichmann. I didn't attend the rally, and Tania began to think that Marlene was the better choice between evils. It might sound a bit grotesque, but I would have been happy enough to have Tania's preferences directed to me.

Sometimes in politics, you're required to hold your nose and swallow. My strategy for the by-election was to come in second with preferences, ahead of the Lib candidate, Jenny Matic. That way, I'd get Lib preferences if Jenny was excluded from further distributions, and I might just about overtake Tania in the race to that 50.01% figure. Without Tania's preferences, it would be tough. But I was out there every day, making my pitch: "Vote Twentyman for a better world! Vote Twentyman for the sake of your kids! Vote Twentyman for the good of your conscience! Vote Twentyman for free beer every Saturday!" Okay, not that last slogan. Worked like a madman, the ageing Les, putting all his aches and pains aside; pounded the pavements doing the letterboxes. I might have kissed a few babies, can't say I'm above that sort of thing. I said a little earlier that I didn't know why I made the decision to run again after losing in 1992 and 1996. But if I'm candid, I know why I ran again. I ran because I love it, all the hoopla, the speeches, that surge you get in the course of the campaign that makes you believe you can do it, you can win, you can stand up on the dais and accept the gold medal. I'm a political person down to my toenails. And it's good for your soul to see how your mates rally round. In a way, an election campaign for an independent is like a celebration of friendship. "What can I do to help, Les? Stuff letterboxes, maybe? Need someone to hand out how-to-votes? I'm with you, brother." I made a point of telling my readers all about the hard yakka of a campaign, and so it is, but by God, it's fun, too, and thrilling.

I didn't win. Marlene's primary vote came in under 50%, way down on the last election, which meant there had to be a distribution of preferences. Jenny Matic of the Libs had finished just ahead of me, so the first distribution went to her and to Marlene, and the preferences were just barely enough to get Marlene over the line. I ran miles ahead of any other independent, as I had in the other elections I contested, but didn't get the cigar. At least my candidacy threw a strong light on the crying need for more youth-at-risk resources. And not just money and manpower, but actual *concern*. By which I mean something that comes to life in the hearts of people; something that makes them embrace the idea of keeping kids in school, keeping kids out of gangs. Money, sure, but genuine concern is equally important. If you care about kids in danger of leaping head-first into a maelstrom that will leave them battered and scarred for life, that's something that's done your soul some good. It's our society I'm talking about. I want people to be proud of all that we do to create a good society, in just the same way that they take care of their own household. Every kid at risk, every kid in danger of fucking up something rotten—that's your kid.

19

Love and Marriage

It might sound as if the hurly-burly of youth work didn't leave me any time for romance. No way. I've been married not once but twice, and have earlier in this chronicle mentioned my first wife, Margaret. It was a pretty good marriage, but it didn't last. Three years. Did all the required stuff—sat down to meals together, most times. Kissed, hugged. Fell asleep on the sofa side-by-side watching telly. Argued about whose turn it was to cook, who was supposed to plunder the supermarket at regular intervals, take out the wheelie bins, mow the lawn, bring a cuppa to the other partner in bed in the morning, clean out the budgie's cage, be given access to the car on any particular day. I have to tell you, I can understand how a bloke might get fed up with all the rigmarole of the married state and apply to the court for a decree nisi, but I could never respect a bloke who'd abstained from marriage completely. Bloody hell, you have to get married. You have to give yourself the experience of it. Loved Margaret, she loved me, said sweet things to each other, and yeah, I brought her a cuppa in bed in the morning, as I recall. Did I? Pretty sure. Then I wore out my welcome. Might have stopped out with the boys sampling the amber liquid longer than I should have. Might have neglected an anniversary or two, or three. Whatever it was, the time came when we looked each other in the eye and agreed to go our separate ways. It wasn't a long innings, I must admit. Didn't get to the anniversaries celebrated with gem stones—ruby, sapphire, diamond. But created a bit of happiness, short-term. Once we'd parted, I remember thinking: "Done that. Been married. No need to go to such extravagant lengths again, Les, my boy."

And I didn't, for a time. Satisfied myself with more low-maintenance relationships: Sally and Susie and Betty and Babs and Jenny and Jilly. (Not their real names, in case you were wondering about the alliteration.) A difficulty in romantic relationships for a bloke in my line of work is that I'm often enough on call. The people I assist come to treat me with consideration, yeah, but they don't go so far as to get themselves in strife only during my daylight working hours. I'm often down at the cop shop or at out-of-sessions hearings by magistrates at bloody inconvenient times. Let's say Les has settled down with Susie or Sal to a candlelit dinner starting at eight in the PM, got a couple of strolling minstrels playing lilting melodies on violins, or maybe Barry White on the hi-fi, rose petals strewn along the path from the dining table to the bedroom. Just as the oysters are being served, my mobile rings. It's a cop calling from the Sunshine nick. "Les, I've got a kid down here nabbed on his way out of a 7-Eleven with a shelf full of chockies in his pockets and a Glock G43 in his belt. Says he needs to see you urgently." And me: "Yeah, yeah. Hold on. Be down in ten minutes." Only so many times Susie's prepared to cop this before she says: "Les, go away". It's the same thing for the gendarmes, for detectives. Disruption of home life, come home from a crime scene with nightmarish stuff in the noggin. A fair bit of nightmarish stuff in my caper, I have to tell you. Not good for your sleep patterns to be looking into the eyes of a fourteen-year-old girl whose mum's been hawking her about to grunting boofheads, when the time comes for your head to hit the pillow. Ice addicts going gaga with paranoid delusions—that sort of thing. You learn to compartmentalise this shit for the sake of your sanity, but it doesn't always work. I've been known to cry my eyes out.

So, the Susies and Sallies—some good times, some indifferent times. Then one fine day I met Liz, a fine figure of a woman. Where did I first meet her? Can't recall. Just a friendly hello and a bit of banter. Later in the day of this first meeting, I'm motoring along with my comrades, including Mike Good, in an open-top Mercedes when we pull up at the lights suddenly and the champagne in my glass jumps into the air and lands on the driver of another open-top beside us. And the driver of that open-top, as fate would have it, was Liz. Not best pleased, Liz. Quite a few folk of marriageable age are on the look-out for omens that predict the path ahead of boy and girl. Having yourself drenched in champagne by your future boyfriend maybe doesn't bode well for romance. But Mike apologised on my behalf with flowery phrases, reeking of sincerity and managing to get Liz's phone number and promised that he, or I, would be in touch with various items of compensation. Which he did—Mike, that is—extolling my virtues as a gentleman who was normally courteous and reliable in all weathers. Thus sweeting everything for my next meeting with Liz, fated to unfold in the Domain, outside the Botanical Gardens. I was coaching the East Brighton Footy Club in those days—1982—and I had the boys running the Tan at the gardens. Liz was with some friends at a barbeque there in the Domain, and we recognised each other. Liz! Les! What are you doing here? Could ask you the same thing. So, you remember me? The fellow who threw a glass of champagne over me—how could I forget! And so on. One way and another, we became, as they say, an item.

We both joined a gym in Beach Road, the Twenty-man muscles back then a sight to behold. Also, very bold and macho in those days. We came back from the gym to

Liz's apartment in Brighton one morning and found the front door open, sounds of someone moving about inside. Nothing daunted, I sprinted around to the back, up the stairs hoping to catch whoever it was inside on his (I was assuming it was a bloke) way out. And so I did—a bloke maybe thirty, dodgy of appearance. I said to him: "Who the fuck are you?" He said: "I was just visiting a friend. Let me go, I'm a nice person, I go to church." Maybe not that last bit. I pushed his arm up his back, marched him into the apartment, told him he was a creep, said I was getting the cops. And waiting for the cops (Liz was with me by this time) I stood over him glowering and telling him to shut up whenever he talked. He managed to get out a plea to be allowed to go to the toilet. I said: "No bloody way. You stay where you are or I'll break your bloody arms and legs." I meant it. Liz wanted to let him go to the dunny, but I said no. The thing is, if you're trapped in a situation such as the one this creep was in, you don't actually need to go to the toilet. Sounds counter-intuitive, but it's only when the tension is lifted that your bladder or your bowels cry out for relief. I knew he was planning something fishy. And sure enough, when the cops came, my bloke reached down and frigged about a bit in the region of his lower leg. I glanced down, and there on the floor lay a blade. He'd been intending to slip the blade into his hand and go me in the guts or somewhere if I'd let him stand up, but denied the chance, he'd wanted to get rid of the knife before the coppers frisked him. As it turned out, he was on the run from the cops in NSW. These days, I wouldn't have the wherewithal to frogmarch a bad guy up the stairs and stand guard over him, but back then, oh boy, I could have upended any bad guy in Australia and hammered him head first into the ground with my bare fists. Extraordinary physical specimen, I promise you. And all for Liz's sole use and delight. Well, for a while. We moved on after a bit.

I remained a free agent romance-wise for a few years after Liz. Thought it best. But doing the bachelor caper needs a little bit of oversight. See, a bachelor can get to be a fussy sort of bugger, pleases himself in his habits, doesn't want to risk any change; at its most pitiable, a bachelor will start wearing upholstered slippers and a flannelette dressing gown, take to placing things in a particular place in the fridge, become a bit Obsessive Compulsive. Once you start wearing super comfy slippers and a flannelette dressing gown, nothing good can happen to you for the rest of your life. It's a fact. That's on the one hand. On the other hand, your bachelor can begin to take the liberties of the live-alone, such as farting at leisure, leaving the cap off the toothpaste, only washing the dishes every third day. Unsavoury. My bachelor habits hadn't reached any sort of dire level when I met Cherie one fine day down at the pub, but all the same, I could see a few danger signs (had taken to admiring the comfy slippers in Target) and I really needed to think about entering the conjugal state once more. It was no more than a friendly chat that day at the pub, but three months later, Cherie gave me a cooee when she sighted me at the supermarket in Barkly Street. We renewed the friendly chat, took it further, went on a date, found we enjoyed each other's company. And married. Lovely. Felt immediately I'd done the right thing.

Cherie later took charge of her granddaughter, Lotus, a lovely kid. So, I became a stepfather. Well and good—a new experience in life, being a stepfather. I thought: "Roll up your sleeves, Twentyman, and do this properly".

She's lived with Cherie and me ever since, has Lotus. God knows what Cherie and I will be facing over the next few years of parenting, but whatever it is, bring it on. It's one thing to be out and about in my outreach role, finding places for kids in strife to live, bustling them along to school, into basketball, but here I am taking my own advice in regard to Lotus. And what I want for her is exactly what I want for every kid who comes my way. Love and support at home; off to school five days a week; hobbies and pastimes that do not include gear and gangs. See to it, Les.

Your relationships—marriages, friendships, love affairs—are largely the measure of your character. Life puts you face-to-face with women and men and asks you to show what you've got. Sure, you can become a hermit if you like, but being a hermit is not entirely human, don't you think? You have to get in there and embrace the rough-and-tumble of life. I've been made glad and been enriched by my relationships. And yeah, I'd be willing to be judged by the sum and total of the way I've loved and reached out, and been loved. Don't know who'd be doing the summing up, but whoever it is, let that person say: "Les Twentyman, yep, he lived a life, all right."

20

Gum

You've heard of Gum. Probably. Right now, 2017, in his early twenties, he's in the process of becoming a superstar. Gum had a fairly good chance of becoming something else altogether—maybe a gang chieftain, something like that. Well, what do you think? A kid from Sudan, fourteen when he came to Australia as a refugee, planted out in the wild west of Melbourne, feeling alienated by racist taunts from the other kids around him? Yeah, a good chance he could have ended up in a gang simply for the sake of his self-esteem. We (in 'The Twentieth Man') came to know Gum when he was referred to us by his school at the age of fourteen. A bit of anti-social stuff, no big deal. First time I saw him I thought: "Nice kid, something special maybe". A lot of kids who get into gangs, they've adopted this chip-on-the-shoulder thing that keeps their resentment simmering away. If you've got no resentment in you, you're not going to make it in a gang. It's the default mind-set of gang members. You're resentful because you're poor, or because you're scorned as a black man in a white culture, or because the Jews own everything, or because people from somewhere in Asia or the Middle East are trying to take over the Wide Brown Land. Resentment is important because it gives you the motivation for revenge, usually on society itself. In Gum's face, zero resentment, but a certain amount of hurt, which is what resentment grows from. Once resentment kicks in, your ambition for yourself is going to decay. Maybe you can imagine yourself happy and occupied in building a life, making something of your talents, but if it gets way too hard, you're going to look at alternatives. Such as doing something especially destructive in a gang.

As I say, no mean streak in Gum, no bitterness, no lust for revenge. He wanted relief from the loneliness and isolation of his life in this foreign land, he needed to feel connected. Gum spent almost twelve years in a huge refugee camp in Kenya while civil war tore the towns and villages of his country to pieces. Strange to say, he was more at home in that camp than he was in the first few years in Australia. You can die of hunger in a refugee camp, or of any of a dozen diseases. You won't die of hunger in Australia, and you won't die of any of those dozen diseases. But a refugee can feel a sort of spiritual death at the loss of a culture, of all the familiar sights and sounds that he carries in his soul. Coming to Australia was Gum's first ever experience of being in a small minority of black-skinned people, and he struggled. People who knew bugger all about him formed opinions on his status as a human being after just a glance. There was next to no support for Gum when he landed in the western suburbs and very little prospect of employment. My mate, Jim Markovski, got Gum into The Twentieth Man Back-to-School program and encouraged him to stick with education (Jim, I have to tell you, is a genius at what he does) and hop into our Redskins program. He thrived. It wasn't simply having an outlet for his energy and intellect; a big part of Gum's turnaround had to do with meeting people who cared, who actually believed he should be given a chance in life. It's something to hold onto, feeling confident that people want you to succeed.

Gum had witnessed bloody horrible shit in his home country, enough to make him sick-at-heart forever unless he experienced kindness and goodwill from some other source. He had his mum, his grandma, and his brothers and sisters with him in Australia, sure, and his mum's love was a big, big part of his survival. But he needed to feel that he could make his way in the community around him. Jim and the Twentieth Man programs gave him that foothold. He kept up his commitment to school, graduated, went on to earn qualifications as a youth worker. And grew taller and taller, stronger and stronger. Brimbank Police took him on as an advisor on African issues, and Twentieth Man engaged him as a youth worker, mentoring the younger kids coming into the Redskins. Boy oh boy, you should have seen him on the court, the way he nurtured those kids. You could feel the good he was doing. The Sudanese kids, the Somali kids, they suddenly had a role model, someone they admired who didn't have to rely on aggression to make an impact.

In my game, you get to see the way in which the goodwill you show to one person can become the foundation of communication with another person. It's passed on. Gum's mum and grandma passed on their love and their values in life. Jim and I and the Twentieth Man folk passed on our respect to Gum, showed him we were ambitious for him, and offered him a path. Gum passes on those same things to the kids he helps and mentors. And those kids, we hope—some of them—will pass on what Gum has given them. It's true that Gum is exceptional. You're not going to come across more than one or two Gums in your lifetime. But I'm not hoping that Gum will become the mould of a thousand more Gums, just that he'll impress the kids he helps. It's all to do with imagination, as I've said elsewhere in this Journal of Les. Gum makes kids imagine something they couldn't grasp before they met him: namely, that a life of cooperation is likely to be much, much richer than a life of aggressive disdain. I mean, if we want any sort of fulfilling life, we have to build it, all of us. Gum shows his kids how to build. Listen to this rave review of Gum's influence that came to my inbox:

You may recall our meeting at Percy's some weeks ago, where graciously you were guest speaker and we had a few cleansers at the bar into the early evening. My local involvement is with the Yarra Wildbeasts Basketball Team and I was pleased last night when at home my 15 y.o. son Lachie told me that his Xavier team was playing a social justice match versus the Redskins today—so I enquired of our boys to see if any of them were a part of that team and discovered that Lino and Deng Dut both played, Lino apparently scoring a windmill dunk at one point on the game—though at 6'8" that's not too hard.

On to the point—Lachie was very impressed I assume by Gum who spoke to the teams and those in attendance about his trials and tribulations in his journey to Australia. As I understand he presented on behalf of the foundation and much credit must go to him as Lachie texted me immediately after the event, a big positive for a 15 y.o. who would normally mutter his comments a day or two later.

I was also sorry to see that from press bereavements I think you lost your mother recently for which I'm saddened for your loss and hope she lived a fulfilled and contented life—though perhaps that's not so easy with a son such as yourself—always on the caper.

And that was from Steve Earl, one of the partners in Harrington Earl Real Estate across the way in Clifton Hill. Top bloke. And good judgement about Gum, wouldn't you say?

21

Final Score

It's been said by learned people with big brains—psychologists and folk in that sort of caper—that human beings have an inbuilt appetite for passionate commitment. Pretty much borne out by my experience in life. At the same time, there are plenty of ways in which passion can go wrong and do harm. I've known Aryan Brotherhood people, neo-Nazis, who hold dear the right to make life difficult for folk with dark skin, and for Muslims, and for Jews. Yeah, they're passionate, all right. Did you ever see any footage of Adolf shouting out his message to audiences in the tens of thousands? That was the message adopted by the Aryan Brotherhood. Essentially: "All Jews must hang". Or in the words of Australia's neo-Nazis: "All blacks must hang, all Muslims must hang, also any remaining Jews". Passion. Be wary. But there's good passion, too. Erotic passion, romantic passion—often does a certain amount of good, but the subject is a little bit beyond the scope of this sober memoir. Sporting passion—that's more in keeping with the Chronicles of Les.

I've coached sides—sometimes both played and coached—and felt myself heading towards the frontier of madness with the lust for victory. Thank God for the rules, because without them you'd suffer a rush of blood to the head and throttle someone with your bare hands. The rules rein in excesses of passion. But let me tell you that the feeling of closing in on victory on the sporting field is one of the greatest feelings in life. And when you hold up that premiership cup, you don't have to thank God because you *are* God. So much for emotions on the field. Off the field, passions raging all over the place at a game of Aussie rules; up in the grandstand, in the cheap uncovered seats and the even cheaper standing room sector, that equal anything the players experience. The fans, mate, the fans. Boy, do they feel it. Now, some fans I can't be bothered with. That's to say, the fans of all AFL teams other than those of the Western Bulldogs. Good people, no doubt, but nongs at the same time. I'm not going to spring any sort of surprise by admitting that I'm building up to a celebration of the glorious result of a game of Aussie rules held at the G on the afternoon of October 1st, 2016. The Western Bulldogs played the Sydney Swans in—what do they call it? Gosh, I've forgotten. Is it the Grand something? The Grand Contest? The Grand

Display? Oh, that's it—the Grand Final. Let me record the final score of that fabulous game on that fabulous day: Western Bulldogs—13.11; Sydney Swans—10.7. When the Bullies last won the premiership, the great Teddy Whitten was still a young bloke with lots of pots of the noble product yet to swallow (fond of the chilled article, Teddy), thousands of jokes still to crack, and a fair bit of mischief still to wreak. I was six, and a follower of the Scraggers. I was still a follower in 1961 when the Scraggers of Footscray faced Hawthorn in the Grand Final, and lost. You've never seen such public ecstasy as the Footscray community showed in 1954, nor such dejection amongst supporters seen up and down Barkly Street after the 1961 result. The Bulldogs are a community, more so than any other club in the league, more so even than Geelong where the economic status of residents is far more mixed than is the case in Footscray. In Geelong, you can admit in public that you care more about sailing or stamp collecting or lacrosse than for Aussie rules without anyone gasping in disbelief. Not so in Footscray. The assumption is that everyone in Footscray loves Aussie rules, and that everyone barracks for the Scraggers.

Why people should identify so powerfully with a team of twenty-two players fighting to take possession of an inflated leather ball in order to kick it between two upright posts 6.4 metres apart is a mystery. The supporters in the stands never touch the ball, never kick it, never mark it. Most would be duffers at the game if they attempted to play it. And yet a loving loyalty develops amongst barrackers that can be more intense than any other relationships in life. The success of the team, or otherwise, lifts the fans up to the top of Happy Mountain, or casts them into the pit of despair. And it's the same, of course, for soccer fans, for rugby fans, probably for followers of camel racing. What the barrackers are hoping for is the euphoria of victory, and when that victory comes in the Grand Final, then boy, that's paradise.

And it's best if you've suffered for that moment of victory. Best if your loyalty has been put to the test. Best if you go to the ground for the first game of the new season with renewed hope and conviction in your heart after the bitter disappointment of the previous season, or the previous ten seasons, or if you're a Bulldogs' supporter, the previous sixty-one seasons. You remember what the New South Wales premier, Neville Wran said about barracking for Balmain in the NRL? "You have to have a big heart." Well, same goes for Footscray supporters. A heart as big as Everest. And the loyalty of that red dog that sat on a tucker-box five miles from Gundagai. And the resilience of Plastic Man. Because, mate, have we had some heartbreaks.

Footscray has never been fashionable, unlike Fitzroy, say, once a battlers' suburb, but boy, did that change. If you come from Fitzroy these days, you know what that means? That your coffee of choice is a long black with skinny soy milk, and that any cake you choose from the counter display will be gluten-free, sugarless, dairy-free. In other words, you'll be a hopeless wanker. Even Collingwood, a working-class suburb in the old days, is now a town where you'll pay a million bucks for a house once occupied by a Catholic family of sixteen kids living on porridge and turnips. House prices are rising in Footscray, I have to admit, but it's still a diehard working-class suburb. You hear people from other places taking the piss out of Footscray folk all the time, and our daggy sense of fashion. 'Footscray Florsheims' are ten-dollar moccasins from Target. And we're thought of as one big brotherhood of petty crims: the standard Footscray car door key is said to be a thirty-centimetre steel ruler. Footscray folk don't care. They know that they have something that Fitzroy is never going to have again: a footy club. Ross Oakley sent a posse to monster the Footscray board in 1989, demanding a merger with Fitzroy. The response of supporters of the club was to send out a Mayday call—huge success, gathered in a million and a half bucks to meet the club's immediate debts, shook cans, carried around blankets at games for supporters to chuck in whatever they could afford. And told Ross Oakley and his thugs to do something crude with their merger plans. That fundraising saga showed the football world what the Bulldogs supporters were made of; it showed them a community prepared to give all they could back to the club they loved. You'd agree with that, surely. When the frighteners from the AFL were sent to put the hard word on the board of the Fitzroy Football Club back in 1996, the leadership capitulated, packed their bags and trooped onto the plane, players included, bound for Brisbane.

I've spent most of my working life out in the west, a big part of that period in Footscray itself. It's made me the man I am, the West. I smell of it, I talk its lingo, and yeah, I look like the west, which is to say, less than beautiful, but very serviceable, solid, never been known to order a gluten-free anything and I take my coffee without any Fitzroy frills. And like almost everyone else in the west, I've only been to the top of the mountain a couple of times in my life. I've never led in the winner of the Melbourne Cup, never been awarded a Nobel Prize, never scored a century in the Boxing Day test. But I've won a premiership with Willy, and I've seen the Scraggers do the impossible and win four straight finals finishing up with the Grand Final and the flag.

I didn't go to the game. I had a ticket from a mate, but he could only get one and I wanted to watch the game with Cherie and Lotus and Cherie's mother, Margaret. So, the three of us took ourselves down to Whitten Oval to watch the game on the big screen. A crowd of thousands congregated, as many as ten thousand—little kids in red, white and blue all the way up to octogenarians with Zimmer frames. It felt as if the community had gathered for the Second Coming. And I swear, if Jesus Himself had appeared at the ground, he would have been wearing a Bullies scarf. Man, the smiles, the happiness. I shook hands with a hundred people, introduced Cherie and Lotus to folk I hadn't seen for years, amongst them, for sure, kids now grown to adulthood that we'd helped out of strife over the years. I was as high as a kite with sheer gladness. But at the same time—and this might sound odd—I was eaten up with anxiety. I've been a coach, and more than most people, I know how hard it is to win a Grand Final. Things the team has done so well all year have to improve even further in the Grand Final. It has to be 10% better than any game you've played all year. What usually happens in Grand Finals is that one side manages that 10% gain, and one side doesn't. I didn't know for sure that the Scraggers could find that crucial Grand Final improvement. The claw in my guts was not to do with me, but with all these smiling, laughing, decorated fans. I just couldn't stand to see grim disappointment replace the smiles.

So, the toss of the coin, the national anthem, the opening bounce. And the claw in my guts. I could barely see the screen. At half-time, I said to Cherie and Lotus: "Can't see a bloody thing. Let's go home and watch on the telly." So, we did. Our house was only five minutes from Whitten Oval. But even at the house, I couldn't watch. I was like this as a coach. Often, I'd turn my head away, or cover my eyes in a tense, close game. Not watching had become a superstition. Cherie came out on the verandah every so often to give me progress scores. The Bullies kept close to the Swans, then took the lead, lost the lead, took it back. I'm praying to a God I'd barely acknowledged up to then, being a bit of a fair-weather friend of Our Father, but bloody hell, I believed in him that day out there on the verandah. And Allah. And what's-he-called, the God of the Jews?—Adonai, yeah Him, gave Him a bit of a hoy, also Buddha who'd have been a Bulldogs' supporter if he hadn't been dwelling in some supreme state of enlightenment. I was whispering as I paced up and down: "Come on you Bullies! Do it! Just do it!" About five minutes from the final siren, Cherie came out wreathed in smiles. "We're winning. It's ours." I still didn't dare to look. "Come on you Bullies! Listen, God, if the Scraggers win, I'll say one thousand Hail Marys and one thousand Our Fathers. Approximately." Ninety seconds left, and Lotus called me in. Oh, boy! The players were already embracing. Ninety seconds to go, and there was no way the Swans were going to kick three goals to steal the game. I was watching something that hardly ever happens in sport. It was like the Yanks beating the Russians at ice hockey in the 1980 Winter Olympics—the 'Miracle on Ice' game. It couldn't happen, but it did. The Bullies had found the grit and craft to beat a team they should have had no chance of beating.

Over the next few days while I was out and about in the Footscray community, also in Sunshine and in Braybrook, all you could see were huge smiles on every face. Paradise had come to Barkly Street, Suffolk Road, South Road. It damned near made me cry for joy. This community, belted from pillar to post over the decades, the butt of a thousand jokes, transformed by this triumph. People in the west had earned this with their loyalty, their commitment and their grit. When fans call themselves, 'supporters', often all that means is that they go about singing hosannas when their team wins. But Bulldogs' fans support their club in the literal sense of the word. They saved it from extinction. They invested their optimism in the Bulldogs. When I was a kid, my first experience of a community was the community of my household—Mum, Dad, us kids. I've honoured the idea of 'community' ever since. Having a footy club in your community—one that you've put your money into, and your dearest hopes—gives you that much more to savour on a day like October 1st, 2016. I wanted those boys to win that game with every part of me so that I could say to the kids who come my way for help: "You want to know what it means to belong? You want the best feeling that's ever going to come your way? Get your gear on, get out on the oval, get out on the basketball court, play your heart out."

Oh, and the Hail Marys and Our Fathers? On the back burner. I'll get around to it sometime before the bounce of the ball for Season 2017.

22

Gala

Back a few decades when we first dreamed up the Les Twentyman Foundation, our ambitions for its future were humble, I promise you. That first year we sat a few homeless kids down to a Christmas dinner at my mum and dad's place, filled their bellies, popped a few of those cracker things, sang a song or two—'Oh come all ye faithful …' That sort of thing. Jim Markovski, Ron Coleman and Les—we were faithful, you could say, not so much joyful and triumphant. It was like a scene from a Dickens novel— three knockabout blokes with good intentions, half a dozen urchins, a few tears of gladness, mostly mine. Yeah, well, time passed and the Les Twentyman Fund was able to do a bit more good the next year, more the next, and soon had more urchins at what became the annual Christmas Party than you could count. Can be a bit of a chore for the staff to organise the whole thing, but I can tell you from the heart, it's worth every minute of exertion to have kids coming up to me and Jim in the midst of the merriment to say: "Thanks for this, Les. Thanks for this, Jim." When the kids say that, they mean to thank the whole outfit, not just me and Jim.

These days, we stage an Annual Gala in October, well before the Christmas Party, to celebrate the achievements of the Fund (or the Les Twentyman Foundation, as it's now known—you read the chapter on the establishment on the Foundation, didn't you? You haven't been skipping chapters?). I say, 'to celebrate the achievements of the Fund' but what I really mean is 'to celebrate the achievements of the kids'. We send out invitations to all of our sponsors, and to some of the kids we've assisted, the less shy ones, ask them to jump up on the stage and share their experiences with the rich and famous. And the not-so rich, the not-at-all famous. Anybody passing the event—usually held somewhere glittering and gorgeous—might think that it's just a touch ironical that the battlers of the western suburbs, kids especially, are being honoured in an upmarket suburb with Moet & Chandon and Black Sea sturgeon. But the guests pay plenty for the nosh, and plenty more when we hold our auction of donated items: works of art, jewellery, books signed by their authors, bric-a-brac, ballgowns, vases, holidays to tropical lands, dinners for two at fabled restaurants, a massage with guaranteed spiritual benefits (no kidding!), and so on and so on and etcetera. The gala raises tens of thousands for the Foundation. It's become a red-letter item on the calendar of the well-heeled—those with a social conscience, at least. Here's the thing: a big percentage of the well-heeled do actually *have* a social conscience, and it's genuine. They're not about to make a bundle of all they own right down to their under-junders and drop it in the lap of a beggar on the street, like St. Francis of Assisi. But yeah, they want to help, they really do. It comes down to a choice of the type of human you want to be. Nothing easier than to enjoy your bounty and dismiss the fucked-over kids out there as someone else's problem. But our people, our sponsors, those who come along to the gala, they can't do that, any more than I could all those years ago when I looked at abused kids with sorrow and pain in their eyes that kids should never know. And it's got nothing to do with wanting to feel good about themselves, embracing a charity to relieve guilt. It's simpler than that. They want the suffering to stop. That's it.

The Gala of 2016 was held in the convention centre of a fancy hotel in Queens Road just across the way from Albert Park, 30 tables each seating ten guests, a small army of attentive waiters and waitresses hovering about with bottles of Penfolds, ready to refill your glass as soon as you'd sipped. We'd chosen an African theme for the evening to acknowledge the big number of immigrants from Somalia, Sudan, Kenya, and Ethiopia, trying to fashion a life in the western suburbs. We hired an ensemble of South African musos to entertain the crowd—Zebra Zone—very energetic, a couple of drummers, three dancers, including a guy who launched into a series of back flips from one side of the stage to the other. On a dais up the front of this whole shebang we had an artist, Dennis Jones, big rep, painting a portrait of Nelson Mandala—watercolour I assume since it had to dry quickly. The portrait was to be auctioned as soon as he'd finished it. He was wearing an artist's smock, old Dennis, looking absolutely the part. I'd been draped in a sort of African stole tied at the shoulder, a chieftain's clobber, bloody gorgeous.

We've got Hamish McLachlan as MC, a very witty man, just the right amount of comedy to lighten the message. A big screen to his right highlighted the points he was making—oh yes, very state-of-the-art, the LTF galas these days. Regular reminders from Hamish about the auction, demands for cheque books and credit cards to be kept at the ready. I'm powering my way through the entrée and pausing between mouthfuls to respond to a stream of guests crouching where I'm seated to say gidday. I feel like I'm in a type of *Godfather* scenario with all these folk stooping to shake my hand and murmuring warm words: "Lovely to see you again Les, wonderful evening …"

The Africans returned to the stage after Hamish's rave to leap about with a display of energy that leaves you gobsmacked. After all that hoopla, Ali was welcomed to the lectern, a Sudanese girl of sixteen, tall and slim and beautiful as so many of the Sudanese girls are, dressed in a stylish black outfit. Ali is one of the LTF success stories, terrified when she first landed in Sunshine from a refugee camp a few years ago, felt like she would never find her way into Aussie society, never grasp the culture. But she stepped out of her isolation and dread to join in the Redskins basketball program, and her confidence grew. Doesn't matter where you come from and what culture you were raised in, you can pick up the rules of basketball in fifteen minutes. See, playing basketball demands that you think of yourself as a team member. You have to cooperate; you have to pass the ball if another teammate's in a better position to shoot. And you're going to start taking pleasure in cooperation. Your teammates become buddies, the coach is seen as someone who wants you to enjoy yourself. And hey presto!—the isolation is gone. At my age, you're looking for things that give you confidence in your fellow human being, and a story like Ali's does that for me. Brought tears to the Twentyman peepers.

Other kids from our programs stepped up to the mike and gave a bit of an account of themselves, to the delight of the gathering. Nothing bolsters the conviction of the sponsors more than a healthy, smiling kid speaking of his or her despair-to-joy experiences. Wouldn't be quite so successful if we chose a kid in daggy old jeans, a T-shirt, metal in the nose and lips and a gallery of tatts—and we have kids like that in our programs. So, you could say that we selected the most marketable of the kids in our programs to present to the sponsors. That's okay. You have to show a bit of savvy when you're spruiking for oxfords. And what about me in my fancy suit and collar and tie, hair slicked back, what's left of it, been to the quack for a few doses of Botox, bit of eyeliner, splash of cologne, the most gorgeous version of Les modern science can provide. I'm on display, too. Don't want a figurehead looking like he's just emerged from the The Plough after a session with his comrades.

David Young, our chairman, gave the major speech of the evening, as he did at the launch of the Foundation earlier in the year. Listening to David as he so expertly ticks off the goals we've kicked over the past year, it strikes me that he's one of those people who'd be a bloody stand-out no matter what profession or trade he chose. In different circumstances, he could have become a panel-beater, and he would've been the best panel-beater in Australia. He's a huge Bulldogs fan, is David, and man, was he a happy fella when the Scraggers saluted on October 1st. Actually, he started his rave by inviting everyone at the gala to join in a whopper cheer for the Bullies. Later, he revealed that the Foundation's budget grew to 1.7 million this past year and was likely to top 2 million in this coming year. A huge percentage of that makes its way into our programs, I'm happy to tell you.

It came around to my turn to harangue the audience— the Mouth himself. I slipped off my African stole before I took the stage; made me look fat, and I can't have that. Up at the lectern, I spoke about kids at risk, what did you expect? But I also threw in an extra-curricular episode about going to the aid of a Vietnamese-Australian woman who got herself up shit creek in Ho Chi Minh city without any paddle at all. She was pretty much ignored by Australian consular officials, but I brought enough heat into the media to get her released. I wanted to show the audience that you can't turn off your sense of injustice just because someone isn't a kid at risk. You can't turn off your mouth. That's the great gift God gave me—my mouth. Doesn't win complete approval from everyone, my mouth. But I'm not about to turn mute. No bloody way. Hope it went over okay. Certainly plenty of applause.

Back at the table, I enjoyed one of those moments of gladness that come along every so often. The reason was this: that so many people would come out on a rainy Friday evening to show their support for our organisation. I mean, you couldn't say that all these folk had chosen the most glamorous of the available charities. And it's rare that the LTF can give the sponsors a display of spectacular success. It's hard, dogged work, the ability to overcome disappointment and tragedies. If you're supporting the Arthritis people or the Asthma people, even the cancer funds, you might get some fabulous news one fine day from the lab: "Cure for Arthritis, Cure for Cancer!" Working with kids at risk, you're never going to get that sort of news—"Cure for child neglect! Cure for poverty!" You have to accept that things could get worse, much worse, and that the kid you have some success with today might fall in a heap tomorrow. In a way, the LTF is a charity that demands more discipline from its supporters than any other. You have to hang in there, and keep hanging in no matter what. Maybe we can't make a huge difference overnight, but if we weren't there, you'd see a huge difference of the opposite sort, meaning things would be so much worse.

One of the reasons that we make such a big deal over people like Gum (as I've said) is that he's much further along the road to success than anyone else. Everyone in the organisation knows that there are only so many Gums to go around. So, we throw a spotlight on him, of course we do, as if we're saying: "This is what's possible". We could get all the kids in the Redskins program together and take a wide-angle pic, sure—more than 400 kids of all ages. Or we could gather up the hundreds, even thousands of other kids we've got back into school, and kept there. But we'd have to be honest and say: "And once these kids move on, we've got an even greater number waiting for our assistance". It doesn't trouble me, the fact that we can never say to our sponsors: "It'll all be fixed up in a couple of years and we won't need a Les Twentyman Foundation after that". We'll need a LTF for-bloody-ever, long after I've gone. So, the gladness I spoke about—yeah, it's really good to feel that.

23

Agenda

I'm not always on the beat these days, meaning that I'm not called on to throw off the doona at midnight and race down to the copshop to advocate for a fourteen-year-old kid who's been picked up shoplifting. Or racing to a hospital for some other client who's attempted suicide by drinking a litre bottle of White King. On the beat, my friend—it takes it out of you. I've gone home from these interventions at times shaking my head in despair and knowing I won't get back to sleep that night. The nightmares I've dealt with when I'm called out are—I have to say—are worse than anything that comes my way once I do become unconscious. Vampires, werewolves, monsters—piece of cake compared to looking down at a hospital bed where a kid's been patched up after trying to cut her throat.

So, yeah, I'm off the beat, but bloody hell, I'm kept busy. Look at this schedule the week after the LTF Gala. A call from Bill Shorten, the Leader of the Federal Opposition, after I'd spoken to him at a tour in the west of the city the previous week. I wanted to make Bill aware of our push to get our kids employment with the Coles supermarket at the Showgrounds shopping centre—the supermarket, actually, that Bill himself shops at. Bill said that he'd met with people high up in Wesfarmers—they own Coles—and had spoken to them about our concerns. And the Wesfarmers folk were happy to listen to the scheme of finding jobs. Good result. And I was the guest speaker at the Wingate Avenue Community Law Centre AGM, just off Dunlop Avenue there in the heart of Ascot Vale, a couple of days later, so that followed on neatly.

Later that week, a message came from Randal Killip, the marketing director at Media Stable, to say that he'd sent out far and wide a short piece I'd written on the new synthetic gear coming onto the market:

Swallow one little pill and you are off having the time of your life ... Frakka, Wizard, Zombies. Sound's cool, right? At that moment, there is very little thought given to the sweaty bikers cutting the powder with whatever is nearby. Kids are invincible, so they believe. They might have heard stories but know it won't happen to them. The reality is that our kids are playing Russian Roulette every time they pop a pill or swallow a spoonful of powder. We need to do our best to protect our kids. A good start would be pill-testing machines, widely used in Europe, to be made available at dance parties and schoolies' hotspots, letting kids know in an instant that what they're about to put into their system is not about to kill them, or is about to kill them. The question is this: is our society adult enough for such a solution, because one thing is certain—kids will keep popping pills, and we cannot police this in the way we have been, so what are we prepared to do to protect kids from themselves?

I keep banging away in the way I have for years, for decades, and I don't want to make it sound as if I'm on automatic pilot—you know, a prepared response to every crisis that comes along. But I have to say something for the sake of my own conscience. Look, I'm fucking sick of drugs, and I particularly hate whoever invented ice. But me being sick of drugs isn't going to save a single kid. Can you see what I'm trying to do? I'm trying to create a coalition of people who want to get themselves engaged in more imaginative ways of dealing with gear. Yeah, I want things that are still ten years away—drug-testing apparatus; safe-injecting rooms; decriminalisation of possession; maybe even decriminalisation of drugs altogether—but I have to make myself believe that by banging, on I can make that ten years, nine years, or eight. Because that one year less, or two, will save hundreds of lives.

Later in the week following the LTF Gala, I had a meeting with the Melton coppers to arrange for them to talk with our Youth Work staff about gangs—Apex, in particular—and working with at-risk kids on the Melton patch. You know Melton, do you? Out in the west on the Ballarat Highway, a huge growth area over the past two decades. You can gaze out the window of your car at a grassy paddock as you pass Melton on your way to Ballarat in the morning, then when you return in the afternoon the same paddock will be covered in three-bedroom houses on tiny blocks without enough room to swing a cat—certainly not enough to throw a ball around or put a shed in. No kidding. These boom suburbs on the fringe of our cities attract young families, so there're always heaps of kids running about. In Melton, the young kids have become teenagers, so perfect targets for the dealers that the bikie gangs recruit. And Melton isn't Paris, France, and it isn't Manhattan—exciting places like that. It's just Melton, pretty boring, so if you're fifteen and one of your mates says to you: "Ice, you gotta get some of it into your system, fan-fucking-tastic!" then you're bound to give it a whirl. Different matter if you've got other things in your life. You could be in a Redskins team, a footy team, something of the sort. But a lot of the kids in the west, they're sitting ducks for the dealers, and ideal candidates for the gangs. And when they're hooked on the gear, they confront the hopelessly unimaginative response of our society, which amounts to: "Lock that kid up".

After the gala, an invitation for Handsome Les to speak to the staff at the Malmsbury Youth Detention Centre came, also the Parkville Centre. Both Malmsbury and

Parkville are overcrowded to buggery with all the recent drug arrests. Remember what that kid said about being in the clink? "In here, if you're not in a gang, you're dead meat." Both Malmsbury and Parkville are academies of crime. The education the kids get in these places amounts to an accelerated degree in dealing, in intimidation, in the use of weapons. And yeah, I know, it's an age-old problem. If you lock people up in prisons, any prospect of rehabilitation disappears, but it's difficult to imagine an alternative to prisons. Maybe prisons should be places where prisoners learn a trade, or study. But something has to be done, for Christ's sake. Every time I set foot inside a prison, I have to shake my head at the sheer futility of the whole arrangement. Anyway, at the age of sixty-nine, I'm not about to come up with a workable alternative to prisons, am I? But anyone reading The Chronicles of Les who has any ideas, get them out there, change things. Please. Been in so many prisons, so many, and I've never left one with a good news story.

Here's a yarn from my experience in prisons that demonstrates the point I'm making, and in the cast of characters is one of the most reviled prisoners ever to serve time in a Victorian jail. I was giving a talk down in Marngoneet Correctional Centre in Lara, on the Geelong-Bacchus Marsh Road. Right next door to Marngoneet—a medium security place—is Barwon Prison, a maximum-security jail. In my little audience of eleven prisoners I had a few who had been brought in from Barwon to see if they could benefit from what I had to say. I gave my rave about the way in which locking people up tended to groom them for a further career in crime once they'd served their terms and were released. They listened, the prisoners, and they had a hundred questions to ask me at the end of my talk. One of the prisoners wanted to know why an ex-prisoner could never get a police clearance to work with kids even if his record was free of sexual priors. I said I wasn't sure, but I speculated that the cops were probably against giving a clearance to ex-prisoners to work with kids because one of the Russell Street bombers had, in fact, been a youth worker. One of the guys jumped to his feet and began telling everyone loudly that it wasn't him who'd blown up that car outside the Russell Street police headquarters, it was his mate, Stan. I'm thinking: "Fucking hell?" As it turned out, the bloke who'd loudly protested his innocence was none other than Craig Minogue, who was serving a life sentence for the bombing, and for the murder of the woman police officer who died at the scene. This was whispered to me by one of the guards in attendance during my talk.

I was still in the prison at lunchtime, and who should take a fancy to eating his salad roll next to me in the canteen but Craig himself. I was thinking, "Uh oh". Craig didn't return to the theme of his total and complete innocence as regards the bombing, but instead, gave me a detailed account of the way in which he'd murdered a fellow prisoner by smashing his skull in with a barbell from the gym. He was proud of the murder, Craig was. You don't get much of a chance to enjoy your accomplishments in a maximum-security prison. No kudos for learning origami or for teaching yourself to paint like Rembrandt. No kudos for simply being a nice, kind, helpful guy. But if you've smashed in the skull of some inmate you'd taken a dislike to—yeah, you're going to be respected for that. And feared. So, what Craig was boasting about was one of the very few things he'd done in his life that had earned him respect. You see what I mean about the culture of prisons? If you leave prison a better man than you were when you started your term, you're one individual picked out of a million.

But listen, here's a prison story with a twist I have to share with you. I was out at Fairlea one fine day—that's the women's prison, as you probably know—being shown around by the governor, not a speaking engagement, just a familiarisation thing, something to contribute to my grasp of what some of my clients went through. So, the governor—a bloke—has this and that to say about the facilities, all very instructive.

"And now," says the guv, "how about a cuppa, Les, maybe a scone or two, bit of jam and cream?" Never have to be asked twice to sit down to scones and jam and cream. My mum used to make scones back in Braybrook, a genius at it, warranted an Order of Australia for services to baking. We sat down in the guv's office and were served our fare by a sweet old lady, a prisoner. And she murmured to me as she poured my tea and proffered the scones "Made 'em m'self, Mr Twentyman. And Mr Twentyman, let me say that I admire the work you do, yes indeed, admire it very much." She stood beside me with a benign smile as I filled my cake-hole with her scones, watched me as I jumped into a second helping and a third. "Like them, Mr Twentyman? It seems like it." And me: "Oh, yes, love 'em, love 'em". Once she'd departed, I said to the guv: "What a nice lady, don't you think?" And the guv. "Lovely, lovely." "And what's she in here for, if you don't mind my asking?" The guv took another sip of his cuppa and replied: "Murder. Poisoned three husbands. Has a talent for it."

At the Gala, you'll remember that I mentioned in my speech the case of a Vietnamese-Australian girl, Kate Vo, who relied on my help in returning to Australia from Vietnam after her father abandoned her in Ho Chi Minh City, without a passport. About a year ago, a second family in the west read about my intervention and approached the LTF for help with another case. This one involved a mother, who has Indonesian citizenship, and who took her daughter to Bali six years ago, then skived off to Europe with some guy. The girl's Australian passport has now expired and the mother has demanded half a million dollars from Peter Silva, the father, before she will give permission for the girl to travel back home to Altona to live with him. I wrote about the case to the Foreign Minister, Julie Bishop, and she wrote back. No result.

So now I've had to write to Julie Bishop again, hoping to get some progress:

Dear Minister Julie Bishop,

It has been almost one year since you sent a letter to both myself and to Ebony's Grandmother, Jan Silva. Ebony hasn't been able to return to her home in Altona, Victoria, for almost 5 years because of her mother's extortionate demand for a payment of $500,000.00 from her daughter and Ebony's father, Peter, to secure her written approval.

    My Les Twentyman Foundation was contacted by the Silva family after Peter read of how I was able to get Kate Vo back from Vietnam last year after her father stole both Kate and her mother's passports and fled back to Australia leaving Kate in Vietnam for three months until your department rightly helped me get her a new passport so she could return to her home and school where she belonged as an Australian citizen.

    Minister, my granddaughter Lotus Morrison, who is twelve and who lives with my wife (Lotus's grandmother) and I went to Bali earlier this year with Lotus's aunt and hand delivered a card from all the Grade 6s at West Footscray Primary School, a story written up in the *Herald Sun* and the *Brimbank Leader*, wishing Ebony a speedy return to her home here in Australia. Minister, please get Ebony home for Christmas as her grandparents are elderly and cannot travel these days to visit their much-loved granddaughter.

Kind Regards,

Les Twentyman OAM

Now, strictly speaking, the troubles of Kate Vo and Ebony Silva are outside the brief of the Les Twentyman Foundation. Sure. But what are you going to do if people seek you out and ask for your help in the way that the Silvas and Kate's mother did? They thought I might have connections that would assist them, and I do. I suppose this is the stage you reach when you've spent your life trying to do some good. It's like having a knack for turning water into wine. Not a common knack, but if you can do it, people are going to say: "Les, lemme see you do that thing with the water jugs, mate." And I wave my hands about over the big earthenware urns, and hope I still have the gift. But look at me—now I'm comparing myself to Christ and claiming I can perform miracles. Les, get a grip!

Anyhow, that's the agenda for a normal week on the Twentyman calendar. And you know what? I couldn't retire if I wanted to. Because that would mean retiring from having a heart, from giving a damn. Now, in any community, you don't want too many Les Twentymans. Could be a disaster with more than a small number of folk going about with their mouths wide open, shouting and gesticulating. I admit that. But tell me what you think—is there room at least for one of me? I'm hoping your answer is "Yes", because I'm not going away. I had a mouth as a kid, I had a mouth as a young adult, I had a mouth all through my thirties, forties, fifties, and now in my sixties. I've still got a mouth on me. If I (and my wife) can put up with it, so can everybody else.

24

Spotlight

People, groups of people usually, love to give out awards. You can get an award from the Nobel Committee for one thing and another, writing books, building a better mousetrap, so on and etcetera. And you can get an award—the Ignoble Award, have you heard of it?—for inventing something absolutely ridiculous, like an electric fly-swatter with a twenty-horsepower motor. Comedians, actors, publishers, cooks, dog breeders, butchers, carpenters, motor mechanics, birdwatchers, bakers, illustrators, hairdressers and rhubarb growers—they all get awards. I've won a few myself: Most Handsome Man in Australia, ten years running, 1986 to 1996—that's the award I most like to boast about, naturally, but not far behind comes the Victorian of the Year gong

I was given in 2006. Had the press all over me when the announcement was made. "Les, Les, Channel Seven, Les, what's the secret of your success?" "Hey, Les, *The Age* newspaper, can you perform miracles, Les, raise the dead, stuff like that?" "Gidday, Les, News Corp, how are you going to handle the groupies once word gets out of your award, Les?" I've got a little anecdote for you—my favourite anecdote of all time. At the award presentation, the lady who was acting as MC read out her spiel from a printed sheet: "And now it is with great pleasure that I introduce you to Les Twentyman OAM, Virgin of the Year for 2006!" I had to point out that I didn't qualify as Virgin of the Year for 2006, and that the committee would have to go back to about 1966 if I was pass the virgin test. And even then … well, best draw a veil over all that sort of thing.

A couple of years earlier, I'd been a finalist in the Australian of the Year Award, along with Steve Waugh, Alice Chang, Steve Irwin, Lee Kernaghan, Dr Fiona Wood, Tom Keneally, and a host of other very worthy folk. The Australian of the Year Committee announces the finalists some months before naming the actual winner, and in those few months you get your picture in the paper a little more often than usual. Bit more recognition of you amongst the punters. Now, it happened that I was out at Melbourne Airport during this period, catching a flight to somewhere or other, and as I was going through security, the beeper went off. The security guy said: "Please remove your shoes, sir". Which I did, and stepped through the doorway only to have the beeper protest once more. "Please remove your belt." Removed my belt, holding my daks up with some difficulty. Time was running short for me to reach the departure lounge and I didn't have the chance to fit my belt around my middle again, so I struggled off with my trousers around my knees, my boots in one hand, my ticket in another. I came face-to-face with a bloke who was acting as a guide to four Japanese businessmen, and he recognised me, this gent, having seen my pic in the papers. "That's Les Twentyman," I heard him announce to the puzzled Japs. "He's in the running for Australian of the year." I couldn't dilly-dally and hear what came next, but I like to imagine the Tokyo contingent saying: "Ah, yes, a man who can run with his trousers down, a great achievement".

I've always had a happy relationship with Rotary. They get me along to give a chat at one branch or another, kick in big bucks for the cause. They put me up on a stage back in 2005 and bestowed their annual Paul Harris Award on me; Paul Harris was the American founder of Rotary International in 1905. Then in 2012, the Rotarians issued me a second Paul Harris Award, this one being the Sapphire Award, signifying that the noble Les was being honoured for the second time. If you win it a third time, they give a life-size statue of Paul Harris himself in solid gold. No, I'm having you on. Nice idea, but.

The Save the Children White Flame Award—lovely thing to be given. And the 2015 White Knight Award from a real estate company that takes an interest in community charity work. That award came with ten grand for LTF; very welcome. The Tattersalls Award for 2002 was for the same sort of thing: community involvement, reaching out a hand. And they gave me an OAM back in 1994. Boy, I was chuffed, I can tell you. I've never been able to put any letters after my name, never anything to put before my name, like professor, or doctor. Never expected to. So, it's a thrill to have the right to say: Les Twentyman, OAM. Recognition is important, because most of the time you feel as if you're battling along without anyone having the faintest idea of what you're trying to achieve. Just having a light shone on your work for a short time—yeah, it does your heart good, I have to admit. And better still, if gives a bit of ballast to the Foundation. That can't hurt.

One final award worth mentioning. In a magazine poll of Australia's worst dressed men, I came in second to Richie Benaud. Damned close call. I ran into Richie at the cricket a little while after the poll and thought I'd introduce myself. "I'm Les Twentyman, Richie. You pipped me to the post for worst-dressed man in Australia." Richie gave me a glare, then saw I was harmless and changed the glare to a big smile. But I think my mate, Dennis Galimberti, deserves the final word on my second place on that list. "Les," he said, "you did everything you could to win that award. No shame in coming second to Richie."

25

It Takes a Village to Save a Child

When you reach my age and look back, you don't see a long series of triumphs that puff you up with self-regard. No, you see a big, big cast of people who've supported you and buoyed you up throughout your life; people who've found space for you in the midst of every other damn thing they have to do. And you think: "Bloody hell! How lucky am I?" Because I have been lucky, I've been rich in friendships, and I want all those who've reached down a hand to lift me up to know how glad I am—I mean truly glad—that they came into my life.

Now, 'a cast of people' means that I'm talking about a stage, doesn't it? And if I've got a stage, it means I've got a curtain. And if I've got a curtain, it means that at some time down the way, that curtain comes down for the final time. What can you do? Cop it sweet. But before that curtain descends, let me invite onto the stage one member of the cast after another and shine the spotlight on each one. Harold, would you step out, mate? I'm speaking about Harold Mitchell, the big fella of media buying in Australia, executive chairman of the Mitchell Communications Group and of Aegis Media Pacific. And just as importantly, a philanthropist, who goes about with a big bag of money handing out folding stuff to the needy. Back in 2000, Harold was a guest on Neil Mitchell's 3AW breakfast show and Neil asked him who he thought of as a hero. Harold said: "Les Twentyman". And went on to say kind things about me and my career and my values. I wasn't listening to Neil that morning—usually I do listen, but I might have been having a sleep in, might have had a hangover. But later in the day a mate told me what Harold had broadcast to the citizens of Melbourne. I didn't know Harold at that time but all the same, I found his number somewhere and phoned him. As you would. Phoned him to thank him. Harold wrote an article for the *Herald Sun* a couple of days later repeating what he'd said on radio, essentially: "Les, good bloke, gets himself out there with the downtrodden and demoralised". Been mates ever since. He's there for LTF when we need him, and we always need him.

David Smorgon is one of a long line of Jewish philanthropists—and to me, the most important bloke in that long line—who consider it a duty to leave the world a better place than it was. It's a tradition. It was David and Jack Morris who organised that luncheon in 1992 that raised $374K to build youth crisis accommodation on land winkled out of the railways by Jeff Kennett. David invited people to the luncheon who understood that they'd be asked to throw dough into the hat when it was passed around—and when David expects you to throw money into a hat, you do it. He's helped the cause in a hundred ways over the years.

This one's for my brother-in-law, Stephen Coon, who nursed me for nine months when I was in a wheelchair that time, drove me all the way up to Alice Springs for the Variety Bash back in 2009. Looking out for me in that way called for a lot of patience, but Steve is full of the right stuff. Eternal gratitude, mate.

Paul Wheelton, AM and TB (Top Bloke) has helped us out more than once, more than twice, lots of times, financially and otherwise. Valued mate. What about Alex Siddons, who made that terrific doco about me, *The Westside Watchman*? Me, Les, up on the cinema screen in all my glory? You have to be thankful to a bloke who reveals your beauty to the public.

Chris Byrne, runs Westpoint Ford out at Hopper's Crossing; step into the spotlight, cobber. Chris steps in three times a year when LTF arranges an outing for the kids, could be a surfing safari, could be attendance at an

AFL match; we need the dough to cover pies and ice creams and sangers and sunblock and floppy hats and Aerogard. Three of these jaunts each year and Chris cheerfully stumps up $2,000 bucks each time. What these outings achieve is this: the kids bond; the kids experience a bit of optimism about life for a change, and the kids enjoy being able to trust the adults around them. Mostly a novelty.

What about John Fowler? I met John through the Sandringham Footy Club and we watched a few VFL games together. We do ads for LTF on 3AW together, "Knives trash lives", thirty seconds of anti-stabbing propaganda. The message is that a lunge with a blade lasting two seconds could see one party in the morgue and the other in court, eight to twelve years for homicide, and it's bloody boring in the clink.

Ruth Hewitson, please step forward. Ruth is my mate Iain Hewitson's wife, and this kind woman came to my bedside while I was in a coma, and read the newspapers to me. Bloody thankless task, because I didn't know a bloody thing about it and couldn't even whisper a thank you. I don't know how much discipline you need to read aloud to a rumpled figure in a bed with his mouth open and dribble forming a soggy patch on the pillow, but probably a fair bit. The thing is, brain doctors say that it's good for anyone in a coma to have voices around them. Might have made its way into my comatose dreaming, Ruth's voice. It was more than a voice, of course. It was the concern, and the quiet words urging me to recover. And let me introduce, too, a man who needs no introduction (as they say) Iain Hewitson himself, Big Huey, master chef, restauranteur, and a terrific supporter over the decades. We've enjoyed Christmas dinner at Huey's for twenty years, and boy!—a Christmas dinner fashioned by Huey is a sight to behold. While I was away with the fairies in hospital, Huey donated the meals he prepared for his show on telly to LTF.

The doctors at The Alfred saved the Twentyman bones and body, but after I emerged from my coma I needed someone to save the Twentyman dwelling. A bloody awful mix-up with the banking during my lengthy hospitalisation saw my mortgage balloon into the hundreds of thousands. Somehow or other, the regular payments hadn't been directed to the coffers of the CBA. The bank should have advised me that something was wrong, but it didn't. Dennis Tomaris, a partner in the law firm of Cornwall and Stoddard and a friend of LTF came to hear about the fuck-up and intervened with the bank, fixed the mess, saved the house. And thank God. A homeless man with his family helping the homeless? A bit too much irony in that.

What, I'm inviting Jack Levi onto this stage of mine? Jack Levi who's spent his life on classier stages than mine? You know Jack as Elliot Goblet, his legendary shtick, but what you may not know is that Jack is the force behind 'Comedians for a Cause', a posse of comics that stand up for all sorts of folk, including the kids at LTF. Jack gives his time and talent to raising money for us. More power to his funny bone.

Mark Campbell, who owns East Coast Films, makes ads for LTF, and good on him for that. Gives a professional look to our promotions. The ads I've made without the input of Mark—not so good. Awful. Bloody awful. Mark has been all over the place filming our 'Heroin Without the Hype' series, designed to give people a candid look at addiction, no sermonising.

The union movement makes its entrance. Big gidday to Paul Spears, organiser for the AWU. Paul came up with the bright idea of getting union members to donate five bucks a week from their wages to the Save Our Kids fund (SOK). The fund has provided a hundred thousand bucks over the years to organisations like LTF. Brilliant idea, comrade!

I can tell you someone who isn't here, and that's my blockhead of a stalker. But Rob Stary's here. Rob's the criminal lawyer who helped me get my stalker off my arse, an excellent piece of work. Also, he does pro bono work for us!

My cousin, Peter Gordon of Slater and Gordon—mate, let me focus the limelight on that handsome mug. Well, of course it's handsome, Peter's pan; you know the saying—'Handsome is as handsome does'? Well Peter does every sort of handsome stuff. I got together with Peter in 1989 during the Bulldogs' crisis, and later when the 'Save the Bulldogs' campaign was firing up. Peter was president of the Scraggers in 1989 (for the first time; he became president again in 2012) and there is no more noble office in the world—not even Sec Gen of the UN—than Bullies' president. I was with Peter in his car driving to a Bullies' home game against Fitzroy when he was denied entry to the ground because he'd forgotten his membership pass. "I'm the bloody president!" he complained. The guy on the gate just shrugged, but then he saw me in the back seat. "Is that Les you've got with you? Why didn't you say so!" And he waved us in.

That was me coming to Peter's aid, but later on, in 2007, he came to my rescue when I was leaving Open Family and found myself dudded by the CEO there when she cropped my severance pay by two weeks; she said my mind wasn't on the job. I thought: "Bloody hell" On what basis do you decide a worker's mind isn't on the job? Did the CEO—okay, I'll give a name, it was Sue Renkin—suddenly feel that punitive trimming of an employee's wages is an acceptable option? Peter came to hear about it and fired off a letter that threatened Sue with life in prison without benefit of parole (not quite) and she backed off quick-smart. High noon it was, Peter in the role of the sheriff. Pow. And has been practically a patron saint of LTF ever since, if you can be a saint and sharp-shooter at the one time.

Lloyd Williams, you champion. It was Lloyd who came up with the idea of Christmas hampers for our clients, sponsored by Lloyd's Crown Casino. I'd come to know

Lloyd and enjoy the pleasure of his friendship earlier than the Crown hamper initiative when Paul Gardner (just stand up there in the spotlight to the right of Lloyd, Paul) contacted Lloyd and nineteen other leading businessmen to see what contribution could be made to LTF. Paul was head of Grey Advertising at that time, and had been making ads for us. After speaking to Paul, Lloyd phoned me. "What do you need?" he said. I thought about it for about ten seconds before suggesting a bus to get the kids to their footy matches, or basketball games. "You've got it," said Lloyd, and the next day we picked out the vehicle and drove it back to LTFHQ. The kids were amazed. I was delighted. Lloyd was happy. Our own bus. I thought: "Man, we have arrived".

And now, a round of rowdy applause for three members of the Brighton Rotary Club—Ian Mence, Paul Nicholson and Peter Sherman. These guys run a sportsman's night each year with the takings going to our schoolkids programs, books and uniforms and the like. A pretty penny, I have to tell you—fifteen grand annually.

Alice Pung next, lovely Alice. She's a patron of LTF and she has the distinction of having grown up with her Cambodian family in good old Braybrook. Alice is a writer, one of the best, and she finds the time to pen articles for *The Age* that promote the activities of LTF. The gentlemen already on the stage might need to clear a space for Alice, and also see if you can find a couple of telephone directories for her to stand on. Only about the height of a kitchen stool, is Alice, but boy, she packs a wallop.

Now what the hell have I done here? I've got Lauren Jackson, legend of the hoops, standing next to Alice Pung. Alice's topknot comes up to Lauren's knee. You all right there, ladies? Lauren is a patron of our Redskins program, takes on speaking engagements for us. Wonderful woman, big heart.

Okay, let's have a line of three women by adding Jenny McCrabb in her Speedos, principal of St. Kilda Park primary, also on the LTF board, and we're glad to have her. Jenny got herself in contact with me years ago when I was trying to get the Escape from Alcatraz swim into the headlines. This was a swim across San Francisco bay, from Alcatraz to the shore, three hundred participants from all over the world and each one sponsored. Jenny herself signed up for the splash, and she and four willing blokes trained each Sunday at the Brighton Baths in the hope of building up enough strength to avoid drowning. The swim raised thirty thousand bucks, and the winner was my brother-in-law's son, Jackson. I had nothing to do with it. He was just faster than anyone else, I swear.

Oh, and Alan and Nick—bloody hell, can't forget Alan and Nick, which is to say Alan Johnstone of Penfold Mazda, Penfold Audi, Penfold Holden—Penfold Everything; and Nick Johnstone of Nick Johnstone Real Estate. Alan helps out with our vehicles, and Nick officiates at our auctions, such as the one he conducted on the night of our Annual Gala. Genius of the gavel, is Nick.

Oh, boy. The stage is more crowded than for the big 'Do you hear the people sing?' scene in *Les Mis*. Just squash up a bit, if you can. I have to welcome Kevin Hillier OAM to the footlights, my first patron back in the 'eighties, MC for lots of LTF fundraisers. He's a commentator on Radio SEN these days, writes a column for a local journal of record. And some space too, please, for lovely Ann Peacock, who has overseen the Christmas Day Hampers jolly for years and years, also supplies our Great Big Fat LTF Raffle prize.

He's arrived, the one-time mayor of Sunshine, Norm Buckley in his majestic robes and golden chains of office (borrowed for the day—he's no longer mayor). Norm got me a reprieve from a dozen firing squads as mayor, came sprinting in at the last minute with a pardon. "Don't shoot! Les has been vindicated. Only offence turns out to be a big mouth! Hold your fire, I say!"

Ron Coleman has been a friend of LTF from before LTF existed. That's right, isn't it old mate? Ron, who was a journo with the *Sunshine Advocate*, was there when we started The Twentieth Man with that first Christmas Party for disadvantaged kids. And when Peter Cosgrove, the GG, called in on us at LTF to say gidday, he particularly asked if he could meet Ron, a Vietnam vet. Must be a pic somewhere of Ron shaking the GG's hand. I'll see if I can find it.

Jim Markovski has been mentioned in these pages a couple of times. Jim's the Einstein of youth workers, just has that touch. If they were giving out Nobels for outreach people, Jim would be the runaway winner. I've worked with Jim on the Sunshine Council before he moved to Maribyrnong Council, also at Open Family. You know how they say: "No one's indispensable"? Not true. Jim's absolutely indispensable.

Richard Tregear is the best you'll ever find to handle drug users. We hired him for Sunshine Council back in the middle of the 1990s, and boy!—was that an inspired choice. Richard, get up on that stage and stand straight and tall, mate.

Now, this is awkward. I want to say how grateful I am for the support of Williamstown Footy Club, and the Sandringham Footy Club—the Mighty Seagulls and the Equally Mighty Zebras, respectively. But I can't fit forty more blokes on the stage. Would one representative of each team please take the stage? Good.

Drumroll for the arrival of sporting royalty—Merv Hughes, Dougie Hawkins, Rodney Hogg. Merv and Hoggie help to get our annual charity cricket match up and running, much to the benefit of our programs, while Dougie, a great mate not just to me but to hundreds, lends a hand at our Christmas parties and takes on speaking engagements for LTF. Hoggie and Dougie between them have raised over fourteen grand for LTF. Incidentally, while

Hoggie's up there on the stage, let me acknowledge that it was the Hoggster who coined the most touching comment ever made about me: "Les Twentyman is the most famous nobody in Australia". Brings a tear to my eye. Somebody lend me a hanky. Mine's a bit snotty.

Also, Channel Nine. Just one executive up on stage, if you please, Ian Patterson, the boss. I've had blues with Channel Nine, as I've outlined in this book, but the Channel Nine people came good and reached out to me after my health crisis when the Twentyman bank account was as empty as Oliver Twist's gruel bowl. The producers of Nine News, at the urging of Ian, paid the LTF fifteen thousand bucks to tell the tale of my hospitalisation, my coma, all that stuff. They ran the story over two nights. Generous of Nine News because, really, how much was there to say? "Day one—in a coma. Day two—still in a coma. Day three—what can I tell you? Still in a coma. Day four ..." And Ian has been good to me, good to LTF, in many ways over the years. While we're raising a glass to Ian, let me also thank Nick McCallum, who's helped out a number of times over the years, worked with him in the US on that 'Gangs of LA' opus, and it was Nick who gave me the tip about the gun buy-back scheme in Cleveland, Ohio—the scheme that gave me the idea of promoting the same thing here, in the Wide Brown Land.

John Mousaferiadis, step this way, old friend. John owns the Pelicans Landing restaurant in Williamstown, and any number of other eateries in Victoria and further afield. John made Pelicans Landing available to us for fundraising years ago and ever since, and has boosted us and encouraged us every chance he gets.

Dennis Galimberti next, lawyer, good bloke, known each other for years. He helped set up the Twentieth Man Fund, and jeez, that's going back, isn't it? Yeah, Dennis was there when we were bringing kids over to my mum's Christmas dinner table. Had nothing in mind but bringing a little sunshine into the hearts of a dozen kids from the mean streets, and now look at us. Mustn't forget Dennis's role in setting up the refuge after Jeff Kennett got that land for us. Dennis lends his legal. Ian Patterson, the boss, knowledge and skill to the cause any number of times in a year. A veteran.

Russell Howcroft, who's made himself famous in media and advertising, has lent his time and savvy to the cause time and again. Russell, those 'impossible ad briefs' that form a segment on the *Gruen Transfer* on the ABC, here's a suggestion: an ad that promotes empathy for the whacked-out and fucked-up of our society.

Here come the cops! Well, one cop, at least, Bob Falconer, retired from the force now but was once deputy commissioner here in Melbourne, same in Perth for a time. Bob was on the board of the Twentieth Man Fund, and now serves on the Crime Prevention Council of the state government. One of those coppers who give policing a good name.

And Pat Boyle, DS, now more a scholar of crime than a detector of it, the sort of copper who thinks deep about the motives of criminals, and writes down the result. Pat has furnished me with welcome insights into the mentality of gangs, in particular.

You know where we set up the Twentieth Man Fund all that long while ago? A hint: it was in a pub. But which pub? The Plough, where else! The Plough Hotel, heart of the West. Sitting around a gas heater on a chilly night were Ian Killop, Mike Good, Carol Zimmit, Bronwyn, the noble Dennis Galimberti, already lauded in this farago of a document, Luke Fraser, Ron Coleman and Diane Collins. All of those mentioned, please mount to the stage, except for Ron who's already up there. Do you think we could have a plaque fixed to the wall in the bar of The Plough? "Here, in this room, Ian, Mike, Carol, Ron, Diane, Luke, Bronny, Den and Les established the Twentieth Man Fund after a lively sampling of full-strength ales, both local and imported."

You've heard that comment, 'it takes a village to raise a child'? Well, Les can offer you a new version of that: "It takes a village to save a child". All the people I've spoken about who pitched in to help me over more than three decades you can think of as villagers. Billionaires, like Lloyd Williams; highly-skilled professionals, like David Young; knockabout blokes with big hearts, like Dougie; my brilliant PA Bronwyn Perceval—the hard work, generosity and devotion of all of them are needed to lift just one kid out of a dead-end life. I don't bullshit myself that I could have got anywhere without that village around me. That's why I want to stop just here, the whole village up on the stage, a spotlight on the entire gathering. Les, you mug, you did good with the life you were given by your dear old mum and dad. You can say that without needing to blush. But my message is more important than that. It takes a village to save a child.

Coda

Just when you think you've got it all sorted, disaster. A fire broke out in Little Saigon Market in Footscray at about four in the morning of December 17th, last year (2016). The LTF has a depot in the market where we keep all the textbooks and exercise books and what-have-you for the kids in our programs returning to school in this year. Also, a whole heap of Christmas presents for the disadvantaged.

I drove down to the shops early in the morning to buy something or other we needed for the household—Mars Bars, beer, some crucial item—and didn't know a thing about the blaze until I saw the fire trucks and the flames. I was thinking: "Oh, Jesus". The heart of the fire was bloody close to our depot. What I most worried about were the two homeless women who'd been using the depot to doss down in over the past couple of weeks. No need to be concerned for any other folk at that hour of the morning, but the homeless women—hell, yes. I spoke to one of the brigade boys and was told that there were no women in the depot—they must have had a change of heart about where they'd sleep that night. "But your place, Les, no, that's going to go."

It burned to the ground, the whole of Little Saigon Market. I was watching when the fire took hold of the depot. I was thinking: "Fuckin' hell, the books, eight-and-a-half thousand of them, and the pressies, all that fundraising, all those donation, the goodwill of the public all going up like a bonfire". Broke my heart that had been broken a hundred times before.

You have to have sinews of steel in your heart to do this sort of thing, and the sinews in my heart are not steel. I should have taken up some racket that doesn't do so much emotional damage. Should have become an accountant, a lawyer, a politician; should have sold fairy floss at Luna Park. I thought: "I can't take this". But I did. I drove home with the dishwashing detergent I went out to buy, told Cherie the news, and Lotus.

Later in the morning, after the news of the fire on the radio and the telly, messages of support came flooding in: calls, emails, every avenue of correspondence, good mates, strangers. What I heard from each person I spoke to, and also the message of hundreds of emails and texts, was that a tremendous effort would have to be undertaken to make things right. The books would have to be purchased again; the presents would have to be replaced.

The outpouring of sympathy was one thing, but the pledges of cash and services was enough to keep my cheeks wet all my waking hours. Huge donations from the good and the great who'd been supporters for years, but smaller sums, too, and just as welcome. A call from Bill Shorten, who wasn't even in Australia, but had heard about the fire. A kid came running up to me in the supermarket car park with a tenner to help out. "Here, Mister Twentyman, this is for your charity, and my mum says she was so sorry to hear about the fire."

I was on high rotation in the media. One news show after another: "Les, how do you feel after the fire and all?" "How do I feel? Bloody awful!" Tony Jones, who was filling in for Neil Mitchell on 3AW, devoted a whole program to the fire and the LTF, and very welcome that was, mate. Bill Shorten, on his return from overseas, organised a luncheon at Crown for all sorts of folk with goodwill in their hearts for the LTF, and raised one hundred thousand dollars. Good on yer, cobber! Next time I run for parliament, I'll give my preferences to Labor. Maybe. Probably. Okay, I will.

The management of Highpoint Shopping Centre out there in Maribyrnong, bang in the middle of the inner-west, announced that Highpoint would donate enough presents to replace all those that went up in smoke—a wonderful act of generosity. And we had equally generous support so far as getting the message out, from the *Herald Sun*, from Channel Nine News, and 3AW. When I was interviewed on Nine News I wore a Santa cap, with the pom-pom and all. I had Gum there with me, that big-hearted young man. I didn't actually say "Ho, ho, ho!" but you can see from the smile on my face just how happy I was with the flood of gifts and donations. It was an endorsement of everything we'd been doing over the decades. People were saying: "This mob, we trust them, nothing in it for them, it's all for the kids". As a matter of fact, there was something in it for me. A warm glow all around my aged ticker.

One businessman asked me how much we needed to replace all the textbooks for the Back to School program we'd lost in the fire. When I said it was about $50,000, he sent a cheque for that amount the same day. The Western Bulldogs players and the club got behind us too, which was a great lift to our morale. The unions were generous in their donations: as well as substantial collections from their members, the CFMEU provided us with a warehouse to store the toys and books in, and the AWU—always great supporters of us—donated their labour. Members of the Metropolitan Fire Brigade donated toys and vouchers and money; and the Mayor of Brimbank, John Hedderich, gave us the old City of Brimbank offices to run the Back to School Program from. I have to name the Brighton and Colac Rotary Clubs, for their wonderful donations. But I particularly want to mention the kids of West Footscray Primary School (which my granddaughter attended),

St Mary's Catholic School in Ascot Vale and Williamstown Secondary College, for their donations.

Within a week of the fire, five hundred thousand had been pledged to the LTF by the good citizens of Melbourne and beyond: the burghers, the unions, the men and women in the street. Six hundred kids were fed and given a pressie at our annual Christmas dinner—a couple of hundred more than usual. The terrific recovery we made after the fire reminded me of something important: people don't like to see others struggling and falling by the wayside. It pains them, and the first thing they think is: "What can I do to ease the burden?" Now, that's a fabulous resource for me to work with—the generosity of my fellow human beings. I saw it in Braybrook when I was a kid—the way that the community would find ways to help some bloke who'd lost his job. "Here's a half pound of butter for you, mate." And those half pounds of butter from the community, they made a mountain of butter after the fire. Best job in the world, mine is—accepting butter from the public.

www.ingramcontent.com/pod-product-compliance
Lightning Source LLC
Chambersburg PA
CBHW052014290426
44112CB00014B/2233